it

it

inger christensen

translated by susanna nied

with an introduction by anne carson

a new directions book

The translator would like to acknowledge the gracious and generous assistance of
Poul Borum (1934–1996), and to thank Inger Christensen for her extensive and
invaluable contributions to this translation.

This edition of *it* was published with the assistance of the
Danish Literature Centre.

Book design by Sylvia Frezzolini Severance
Manufactured in the United States of America
New Directions Books are printed on acid-free paper.
First published as New Directions Paperbook 1052 in 2006.
Published simultaneously in Canada by Penguin Books Ltd.

"TEXT, extensions 1-8," and "TEXT, universalities 1-8" first appeared in *Verse*.

"STAGE, connectivities 1-8"; "STAGE, variabilities 1-8"; and "EPILOGOS" appeared in
No Man's Land, ed. Annegret Heitmann. Norwich, England: Norvik Press, 1987.

Anne Carson's introduction and "EPILOGOS" first apeared in the U.S. in *American Poetry Review*.

Library of Congress Cataloging-in-Publication Data

Christensen, Inger, 1935–
    [Det. English]
    It / [by Inger Christensen ; translation by Susanna Nied ; introduction by Anne Carson].
        p. cm.
    ISBN-13: 978-0-8112-1594-7 (alk. paper)
    ISBN-10: 0-8112-1594-6 (alk. paper)
    I. Nied, Susanna.   II. Carson, Anne.   III. Title.
PT8176.13.H727D413 2006
839.81'174—dc22

                                                2006027578

New Directions Books are published for James Laughlin
by New Directions Publishing Corporation
80 Eighth Avenue, New York 10011

contents

it

introduction

> . . . If I could start in total silence, slip into the first sentences, hide there as
> in water, flowing, go on until the first little ripples appeared, almost words,
> almost sentences, more and more. . . .
>
> —Inger Christensen[1]

This must be what it was like to hear Hesiod in the eighth century BC recite his cos-
mogonic poems. Like Hesiod, Inger Christensen wants to give an account of *what
is*—of everything that is and how it is and what we are in the midst of it. In the midst
of what? That is her question.

> It. That's it. That started it. It is. Goes on. Moves. Beyond.

she begins.

Hesiod was an epic poet who lived in Boiotia in (probably) the eighth century BC.
His surviving poems include the *Theogony* and the *Works and Days*. The *Theogony* is a
cosmogony: an account of the origin, genealogies and violent struggles of all the
gods—not only Zeus, Apollo and the usual Olympians but elements and abstrac-
tions like Heaven, Moon, Mountains, Death, Sleep, Starvation. The *Works and Days*
is a practical and moral guide to everyday life as an eighth-century Boiotian person.
Formally speaking, the *Theogony* can be read as a hymn, the *Works and Days* as a
piece of wisdom literature, both standard poetic forms at the time. Addressing an
audience that does not believe in gods or trust the wisdom of poets, Inger
Christensen combines Hesiod's purposes into one pronoun. Her *det* is at once a
hymn of praise to reality and a scathing comment on how we make reality what it
is. The dazzled and the didactic interfuse in *det.* It was 1969 when she published it.
Others were attempting such fusions. Think of John Lennon and Yoko Ono ("Give
Peace A Chance" and the Bed-in in Amsterdam); James Brown ("Say It Loud (I'm
Black and Proud)"); Valerie Solanas ("The Scum Manifesto" and attack on Andy
Warhol); Allen Ginsberg chanting the Hare Krishna mantra at Judge Hoffman in a
Chicago courtroom. Here is a description from Susanna Nied of how *det* was
received in Europe:

1 I. Christensen, "I begyndelsen var kødet." Kronik, *Berlingske Aftenavis*, 18 July, 1970.

On its publication in 1969, *det* took Denmark by storm. It won critical praise and became at the same time a huge popular favorite. It was quoted by political protesters and politicians alike; lines from it appeared as graffiti around Copenhagen; some parts were set to rock music and became esoteric hits. When portions were translated into German, *det* brought Christensen international critical acclaim. Today, over thirty years later, *det* is considered a seminal work of modern Scandinavian poetry. Some of its lines are so familiar to Danes that they have slipped into conversational use. For example, the journal of Denmark's city planners took its title, *Soft City*, from a line in *det*.[2]

Det means "it" in Danish. Unlike Hesiod's Greek, Danish is a language in which you must specify the personal pronoun of an impersonal verb. If Hesiod wanted to say "it is" he would use the verb *esti*: "it" is included in the verb. Inger Christensen must say *det er*. She is immediately involved in knowing what "*det*" is. We are caught in the words we use. So, for her, a cosmogony must also be a cosmology. These terms are sometimes used interchangeably in English, but they are not the same. Cosmogony, from *kosmos* ("cosmos") and *gignesthai* ("to come into being"), refers to the birth of things out of nothing. Cosmology, from *kosmos* and *logos*, means the system by which things make sense to us. Inger Christensen divides her *det* into PROLOGOS, LOGOS and EPILOGOS. *Logos* (in Greek) can mean "word, sentence, story, explanation, reasoning, grammar, rationality." It can also denote "number, calculation, price." From number derives its reference to "measure," particularly a "measure of verse or music." From measure comes its application to "law" and "proportion," to "arguments" before the law court and hence its sense of "plea." All these meanings stream and bite and crackle through *det*. Their organization is complex and, as in a great comedy, the effect is a matter of perfectly timed beats.

Inger Christensen discussed the composition of PROLOGOS in a 1970 newspaper article:[3]

> In the beginning I actually acted as if I weren't there, as if it ("I") were just some protoplasm talking, acted as if I were just something that went along while a language, a world, unfolded. That's why I called the first part PROLOGOS: the part, even if it's only fictional, that comes before the word,

2 S. Nied, personal communication.

3 I. Christensen, *Berlingske Aftenavis*.

before consciousness. Background, starting point, vantage point. Prologue, in the theater.

All the stuff of a world emerges in PROLOGOS, from winter-hardy seeds[4] to city halls to Someone, it all wanders out into existence, a bit dazed, rubbing its eyes. As in Hesiod's *Theogony*, this seething multiplicity steps out of nothing without explaining itself. "First came Chaos," declares Hesiod. "It. That's it," says Inger Christensen. What keeps it all from sliding back into nothing is, for both poets, number. Hesiod's epic hexameters propel his poem forward from generation to generation, containing it against decay or meaninglessness; Inger Christensen's mathematics take hold of her data in a similar way. Each line of PROLOGOS has exactly 66 characters in Danish.[5] The structure of the whole is in eight sections:

section	number of poems	number of lines in each
1	1	66
2	2	33
3	3	22
4	6	11
5	11	6
6	22	3
7	33	2
8	66	1

4 The reader may be interested in a dilemma of translation that attaches to these seeds. While I was writing this introduction I was given Susanna Nied's translation in two different versions, took notes on both, then collated my own notes imperfectly. "Winter-hardy seeds" was in the first version I read—and liked, so it found its way into my introduction—but the phrase was revised in the second version to "gemmules." Here is an excerpt from Susanna Nied's correspondence with me on this point:

"... the phrase reflects a mistranslation corrected in the revision: the word that I had originally translated as 'winter-hardy seeds' is actually the scientific term 'gemmules,' specific to the reproductive cycle of certain freshwater sponges. Gemmules are buds that will eventually grow into new sponges. Most sponges' reproductive buds are very fragile, but gemmules have a tough, spiky silica shell that lets them survive freezing winters or other harsh conditions in a sort of suspended animation. Then they continue developing whenever conditions turn favorable. It's one of those exquisite small miracles of biology." [S. Nied, letter of July 11, 2006].

So, long story short, I am most grateful for the defect in my method that provoked this wonderful gloss from Susanna Nied. (Equally grateful, I must admit, that I am not in the translator's position of having to choose between the two phrases and their very different richnesses.)

5 "The English translation retains the original line counts but not the original character counts. . . . Incidentally, Christensen worked out the structure of *det* on a typewriter, before the days of word processing and justified margins. She recalls that setting the manuscript required some creativity on the part of Gyldendal's printers." (S. Nied, personal communication.)

After PROLOGOS comes LOGOS—"the word as creative principle, the place where things are consciously staged, put into action, into relationship."[6] LOGOS has three sections, each with eight subsections of eight poems: 3 x 8 x 8. Here all the stuff that came into being in PROLOGOS moves into a story, that is, into STAGE, ACTION, TEXT. Number evolves into grammar as an ordering device; to shape her story Inger Christensen borrows eight grammatical categories from a book called *A Theory of Prepositions*.[7]

> And then I would have been stymied if I hadn't got hold of *A Theory of Prepositions,* by Viggo Brøndal. His attempt to analyze and categorize the words that languages use to show relationship can be read as applying to the network of relationships that writing builds up as it goes along. From his book I chose eight terms that could stay in a state of flux and at the same time give order to the indistinctness that a state of flux necessarily produces: symmetry, transitivity, continuity, connectivity, variability, extension, integrity and universality . . . [8]

Her choice of prepositions as an icon of order seems a simple but perfect stylistic decision. Any prepositional system implies a philosophy of life. At the same time there is nothing more wistful than these bits of language that solidify all our raw hopes of relation. Such hopes organize Inger Christensen's world as it lies mirrored in her book, groping and longing and headed for death. She incises them into reality as she sees it. At times the hopes are huge and metaphoric:

5

watersteps stoneskies windhouses
aircellars rainhearts sandbodies
cliffmouths riverstomachs icesexes
snowlungs coalbrains cloudfingers
saltnerves eartheyes heartache[9]

Other times they are the size of a body:

6 I. Christensen, *Berlingske Aftenavis.*

7 V. Brøndal, *Præpositioneres theori. Indledning til en rationel betydningslære.* Copenhagen: Munksgaard, 1940, p. 32.

8 I. Christensen, *Berlingske Aftenavis.*

9 LOGOS: STAGE, integrities 5.

8

A society can be so stone-hard
That it fuses into a block
A people can be so bone-hard
That life goes into shock

And the heart is all in shadow
And the heart has almost stopped
Till some begin to build
A city as soft as a body[10]

Or funny:

3

he lunches with the Buddha/stop/must be some new strategy/stop/for one thing they have planted a tree/stop/has not come up/stop/insist they are in the shade/ stop/sunstroke/stop/burns/stop/their lunch invisible/stop/air-knives air-forks/ stop/eating description/stop/emptiness/stop/nirvana/stop/forestall rumors/ stop/eat this telegram/stop/[11]

Or savage:

3

They tie them to the beds when they get restless
No one understands them
The people who tie them seem restless too
They do what they can
When they are relatively calm they sit in the halls
One of them might tell a story
For instance he might claim that the water they're drinking
Is wine Then they all laugh and get roaring drunk[12]

10 LOGOS: ACTION, symmetries 8.
11 LOGOS: ACTION, extensions 3.
12 LOGOS: ACTION, universalities 3.

Or terrible, already gone:

> 7
>
> In the beginning a marked tendency simply to act insane will be noticed in the individual demonstrator. The mere fact that he is naked will cause him to want to hide in the norm of insanity. But as soon as he touches the other demonstrators and they roll each other in the snow or in feelings and get up and pair off and dance and formulate their impressions freely—flowers in their hair and dirt and grass all over them—he will understand that it is a kind of insanity to act as if the individual exists. It is this understanding that must of necessity be disciplined. In order to keep the movement soft at all times, the individual must be hard on himself. Insanity is the ability to do the impossible. Magic is the will to.[13]

After LOGOS has told its harrowing, hope-stained story, after all our prepositions have exhausted their ingenuity, what should come next? Logically, no one can say. After *logos*—beyond words—is a bare place, "comparable to / a worn meteor/ in a totally illusory solar system," she says. EPILOGOS. Life goes on there but it is terrifically formless. We remain in it, of it, accountable to it, but action and risk and "I" are over, creation has run out, the great comedy is ended. "All that is left are days of changeable omen, doomless, with nothing to offer," Hesiod might say.[14] Inger Christensen sees fear everywhere in these days and rolls out Whitmanesque lists of fears driven by their own weird hunger. Beyond words is "fear incarnate." We are creatures who "go out for fear like going out for food." (Odd to find in this epilogue written thirty years ago so clear an evocation of the present day.) Yet EPILOGOS is not a statement of despair. Fear may give rise to "eccentric attempts," she says.

> Eccentric attempts
> when a man
> steps out of himself
> steps out of
> his daily life
> his function
> his situation

13 LOGOS: TEXT, connectivities 7.

14 Hesiod, *Works and Days*, 823.

steps out of
his habits
his peaceful
condition
we call the process
ecstasy
when he claims
that the clouds
shoot by like pain . . .

This pain and its claim, she goes on to suggest, will lead back to words.

It starts
It starts again
It starts in me
It starts in the world
It starts in world after world
It starts far beyond the world
. . .
and there is nothing to do but say it as it is

Where Inger Christensen sees eccentric attempts and ecstasy, Hesiod imagined a bargain with the Muses. At the beginning of the *Theogony* he describes how the Muses met him on the road and asked him to step out of his daily life and peaceful condition:

"You shepherd who sleeps on the ground, you disgrace, you mere belly,
we know how to utter many lies that look authentic,
but we also know, whensoever we wish, to say the absolute truth."
So spoke the eloquent daughters of great Zeus,
and they breathed into me a voice like a god's,
so that I could sing the things to come and the things of the past. [15]

This is the bond into which Inger Christensen enters at the end of her EPILOGOS. To sing the things to come, the things of the past, what it was, what it will be, what it is. What "it" is.

—ANNE CARSON

15 Hesiod, *Theogony*

PROLOGOS

It. That's it. That started it. It is. Goes on. Moves. Beyond. Becomes. Becomes it and it and it. Goes further than that. Becomes something else. Becomes more. Combines something else with more to keep becoming something else and more. Goes further than that. Becomes something besides something else and more. Something. Something new. Newer still. In the next now, becomes as new as it now can be. Imposes itself. Flaunts itself. Touches, is touched. Catches free material. Grows bigger and bigger. Builds itself up by being more than itself, gains weight, gains speed, gains more in its rush, gains on something else, passes something else, which is taken up, taken in, fast laden with what came first, so randomly begun. That's it. So changed now that it's begun. So transformed. Already a difference between it and it, for nothing is what it was. Already time between it and it, here and there, then and now. Already the span of space between it and something else, it and more, it and something, something new, which now, in this now, already has been, in the next now is and goes on. Moves. Fills. Is already enough itself for inside to differ from outside. Plays, shifts, eddies. Outside. And condenses inside. Gains core and substance. Gains surface, refractions, passages, impediments, stimuli among separate parts, free turbulence. Takes a turn, a whole new turn. Turns and twists, is turned and twisted. And pursues an evolution. Seeks a form. Scans its past. Twist after twist takes a different twist. Is picked up to be dealt with again. Turn after turn is rephrased. Gains structure in its ceaseless search for structure. Variations inside fed on matter from outside. Changes character. Localizes needs, divides existing functions into new ones, functions so it can function. Functions so something else can function and because something else functions. In each function a need for new functions, new variations. Reveals free-floating material as catalyst for all that's already too fixed, that's gained its own inertia and lost its tendency toward free combination. Need for new energy for the finished parts. Inexhaustible energy. Alien élan. That's what was needed. Is needed. What gets something else to do something else, something uninhibited. Forces unbridled change. Forces what's sluggish to speed up. Forces it all to happen. It happens. It would never have happened without the alien element. It would never have gone anywhere without the hostile element. It and it and it would have functioned perfectly but without tension or power, without bringing the separate parts, the rules, into play. Without drive. Without confusion. Without mistakes and sidesteps, pitfalls and possibilities. What gained existence never would have gained essence if the essentially different hadn't existed and from its excess doled out death so slowly that it looked like life. So changed, now that it only looks the same. So transfigured. Already much more difference between life and life than between death and life. Already time measurable on the whole only in terms of life. Already the unconditional desolation of space, reduced to conditions. Caught in a provisional game. Reduced to restrained details that ceaselessly single themselves out, divide, differentiate, seek what is different, seek fiction. Revolve, intertwine, contort, turn, rephrase a random turn, bend, double into random expressions, seek an ostensible system. Paraphrase. Feed the great ambition of the separate parts: to work out everything, the universe, in their own little way. All the while wanting to look like something else. Not to look like themselves any longer. Vary so randomly. Diverge by leaps and bounds. Fluctuate, diffuse. Modulate, shade themselves in ways that are themselves modulated and shaded as they go. Haphazardly. Tentatively. Seek a form. Form a form that forms a form. Go beyond that. Maintain a fiction. Seek a non-life that is not death. Play a part. Are unknowable, absorbed in their part, shutting out emptiness. Relate freely to what is alien, hostile, by being alien to themselves. Having it in them. Refer to hostility, uninvolvement, by being involved with it. Imply. Intimate. Build into the rules of the game the inevitable breach of the rules as if it were a rule. As if inevitable death were a natural turn. Needing only to be rephrased right. O death where is thy breach? So changed now that the system catches hold. So free.

It's burning. It's the sun burning. For as long as it takes to burn a sun. As long before and as long after times measurable in terms of life or death. The sun burns itself. Will burn up. Some day. Some day. Intervals to whose lengths there is no sensitivity. Not even a tenderness. When the sun goes out, life (death) will long have been the same as it ever was. It. When the sun goes out, the sun will be free of it all. It. That's it. Meanwhile, in the interim while the sun still has excess enough to dole out death so slowly that it looks like life, life keeps up the fiction. Meanwhile the sun rises, the sun sets. Light and darkness alternate. It brightens, clears, dazzles, is made manifest, only to be obscured, shadowed, cooled, darkened, to slip away. The sky is temporarily sky, temporarily dark. Stars prick out distances and camouflage emptiness, burn for as long as it lasts. Or the darkness is total, the emptiness covered with clouds. Darkness hidden by darkness, temporary night against a temporary sky instead of nothing, reminder of what is farther ahead than the future. Then. Then. For as long as it lasts. In this now. In the next, distance sets in like lightning between darkness and darkness. Electrical discharges, storms, chemistry camouflage stasis. This harmonious memory of nothing, darkness with no darkness, sky with no sky, emptiness with no emptiness missing, this nothingness, this harmony of harmonious harmonies is camouflaged with freedom. Covered by fiction. Kept out of life where the sun rises, the sun sets. As freely as only a conflict formulates its stable model. As downright tenderly, sensitively, as only a life formulates its length, its solitary movements. The sun rises. And in a plain of light the white clouds drift free. In an avalanche of light the colorless mists tumble and condense into watery shapes at home in the world, fixed in shifting color. Flaunt themselves. Move. And are moved. Haphazardly. Tentatively. Seek a form. Find a game. Play a part, shape a game. In a strong steady thermal the sluggish steam rolls across the sky, as if it were a matter of freedom. So it is a matter of freedom. The sun rises, the sun sets. A systematic game. A more real sky.

It hesitates. It finds a place in the world and hesitates in another world. A place, say, the exact place where the Pacific rolls one two three continents into the Atlantic and vice versa. For instance. But hesitates in another world. It rises up, throws itself into beginnings, quickly crests into foam and sprays it forth, spume, refined details en masse. But hesitates in another world. Formulates light in long, undulating cycles, cites the sky in passing, reflects, embroiders brilliant ideas, precolored expressions, but hesitates, darkens, in another world. Goes to extremes, dwells on the glittering surface, lamé, taffeta, sateen. Firms the material. Static, smooth, slides over everything as if it were all. But in another world? Infiltrates glossiness with flecks, sharpens to photosensitive new ecstasy. Crinkles what's smooth, squeezes what's yielding, flings itself outward in flight from itself, the blend of elements. Water and air. Antilight and light, brightness, enlightenment. The sea, overflowing into oxygen and sunflecks, raises a furious sunstorm one calm day, finds the hyperbole of flight and spills into seventh heaven, interference of light waves and water waves, plunges, sinks beneath the surface where the sea lies bathed in a sea of light. But is not burning, is too mortal for that, the Icarian sea. Another world. For instance a world of sounds, mute in its own world, soundless. A surface world buried deep in itself. Or an incessantly gushing, burbling, effervescing world in drugged and silent sleep. A restless, tossing world of anaesthesia, a shining darkness, where light and dark refer to lack of interference between light and darkness. A life far more mortal than that. A(n other) world, functioning as an image of death in the world. So sensitively. Already much more difference between death and death than between life and death. Already space measurable on the whole only in terms of death. The unconditional desolation of absence, confined to existence. Waiting. Hesitating in another world. Caught in an eternal game. Reduced to restrained details that ceaselessly approach, connect, confer, combine, seek density, fiction. Find, for instance, what is placeless. The lethargic sea.

It's come to stay. For as long as it lasts. Has found its final placement. For a while. Gained set forms. (That could have been formed any other way.) Stiffened into set phrasings. (That could have been turned in any other, freer sense.) Arranged itself into standard expressions. (That could also have been expressed in total fluidity.)

Has organized itself, settled, taken place. A world has come into the world. Within the world. Has put its fiction in order. Say, in a world of stone, say in the form of continental shelves, immovable hidden significances, imposing themselves as massifs, manifesting themselves as formations, layer upon layer of impassable permanent meanings, so well-supported, in their own world. Deeper, meaninglessly, in chemical sleep, hushed. That's it, moving, taking place then and now, permanently put to rest. As mica, granite, gneiss. As pyrite, quartz. Suppressed lava, basalt, diabase. Seeking the petrified perspective. Finding solidity in a dazzle of overdone expression. Refinements. Clarifications of cinnabar, zinc white. Gold, silver, platinum. Set forms of cultured pure fictive value. A subterranean game. For instance flickering dark crystals, blindly dispersing their bright colors. Black ruby, sapphire, turquoise. Black transparent glass, diamond. Black white opal. Black whiteness. Subtle structures of organized restlessness, hidden passages between life and death. Invulnerable interplay. In a vulnerable world.

It's come out of thin air, and it spreads, catches on, proliferates, might as well leap into it, leafs out, bursts into bloom and bears fruit. So exalted. Light and CO_2 made manifest in a unique green stance whose dimensions grow. A summer. It catches hold as grass, masks the earth with bracken, secret spores for regeneration, covers it with trees, bushes. Growth. Takes on an expression of covering, though never covering completely. Always with implications, movements in the shade of the leaves. Turns inside out, comes up with veiled allusions to absence, to hostility, ecstasy. Turns to catch up new ways to live out a passion, a passion for green, an overture whose only invulnerability is vulnerability itself. One summer. Does not a summer make. But the summer worn thin that comes back again and again, the summer laid waste that saves up for its next lavish coming, the pollen-dusted summer that rises from the dust, makes death immortal. As if the inevitable had turned inward on its own, as if the flowing veil were actually a flowering, with productivity the vanishing result. A summer defined as winter. Wearing a mask. Playing its game to the end, its double game. In a color-rich duel with itself. Wearing its green cape casually over both shoulders, ready to look like a summer. And repeating: Summer is dead, summer might as well leaf out. Send out its fresh shoots once more to attain full, lush expression, repeat the flourishing decay.

It's come around. Come to stand on its own, confront itself. To disengage from the mass and stand out. It's engaged in an evolution, shifted its stance, attained eminently engaging expression. Has pursued itself and accidentally found itself. As a natural result. Has come to stand for itself. And can begin by itself. To experiment with sets of freestanding, free-floating expressions. Occasionally with straight-swimming ones. Dreaming. In another world. To imply itself. Is what was needed. Is needed. What at last gets it to do something else. Force itself to play the part of something else than itself. As a natural result. To imply that it's alien but ply its alien ways on everything except itself. Alien, hostile, outside. And stance notwithstanding, understanding. At last, has eyes in its head and looks around. Relates freely to a world of stone, for instance, to a world of plants, to air, to water, and to its own world. As another world. At last. Can stand on its own legs and move away from its own death. Is completely free. Though never completely free. Always part of a transformation whose cost is dear. As downright sensitively as only an animal can play out its own mortality. Animated. Forgetting itself. By chasing everything except itself. Forgetting its own death. By killing. Anything, everything. Lighting into its vitals. Feeding on something else's death. Relieving itself of it. Acting as if it only looked the same. Some day. And in another world.

It gets everything in order. In its own world. Co-orders, suborders, superorders. As if it were a matter of a system. Antecedents, postpositives. As if it were a matter of a midpoint. It's a matter of movable insertions, occasional parentheses, the exact degree of irritability that can be called life. Persists. Flaunts itself, touches, is touched. Imposes itself from amoeba to amoeba. Chases random expressions to catch individuality: a specific round vacuole, specific homogenous plasm, strangely split center of energy, in sum the specific life form that constantly systematizes its powerlessness: builds up flagellated chambers, siliceous spicules, gemmules. Encloses several planes of symmetry within a single medusa. Just to die and die.

Just to move between here and there. Just to start some production or other. Brings forth sets of completely identical, completely free, mobile entities, just to move between here and there. Though never completely free. Always just to start the fiction over and over. To keep a life in form. By proliferating. To keep a death formless. Outside the fictive form. Always so spontaneously covering itself with oblivion, always so covertly keeping itself alive between here and there. As if it were a matter of an endless distance. It's a matter of an overcrowded point. Always just where death operates undercover. Though never completely covering. Never without opening the mussel shell and letting the softness vanish. Covertly.

As if the softness, softly vanishing, formless, in chemical sleep, oblivion hushed were all. It. Is all. It. As if it and it and it were less than it. As if even the set expressions, standard turns of phrase, were less than the expressionless, averted, yielding. As if life were less than death. Is less. Is more life defined as death. Can set aside its mask and repeat: life is death. Life might as well get started. Proliferate, achieve a denser formlessness, repeat the fertile formality. The formal difference between starfish and brittlestars; sea cucumbers and sea lilies; flukes, comb jellies, rotifers; lampshells, brine shrimp, barnacles; repeat the purely formal difference between crayfish and butterflies, spiders and fleas.

Repeat: lancelets sea squirts bryozoans, death; lampreys skates sharks fish, vanishing; amphibians snakes, softly vanishing, formless; saurians dinosaurs pterosaurs, hushed, deep in chemical sleep. Is all. Oblivion is all. A spiderweb crumpling in wind; dust flying, yielding, leaving the butterfly's wings gray, withering in the cold; snails choked by earth; beetles, grasshoppers burning; fish drying up in sun, freezing in ice; the standard expressions, torn loose, flutter around, turned to dust, tentatively seek a form, haphazardly find, for instance, formlessness, the place in ceaseless motion between life and death, the place where the unexpressed in the expressionless still finds expression. Loosely. So downright tenderly.

As freely as only a conflict formulates its stable model. As downright tenderly, as sensitively, as only a life formulates its length, its solitary movements. A bird flies up tentatively. Flocks haphazardly follow. Flap around, flaunt themselves. Move, are moved. As if it were a matter of freedom. So it is a matter of freedom: a bird flying up, flocks following, neither more nor less, wings that bear between here and there so freely in the air forced. Never completely free, always in forced formations, wedges, at last to fall and vanish. A bird that falls, a flock that follows. Animated. In an avalanche of life, a life loosely flung off in passing, formed hurtling into formlessness. Just to have lived.

At the boundary, in the endlessly vanishing space between motion and isolated rest, the hidden passages between life and death, in it, what is fleeting organizes its restlessness, distributes functions, develops organs, systems, tissues, skeletons, polishes its routines, repeats the set expressions, the existing order. Functions because it functions, so something else can function, or because something else functions; persists in its impossible, at last consciously futile attempt to withdraw, to grandly outdistance its own mortal danger and stay in the endlessness between here and there. As if there were something to get away from. As if a non-life existed that was not death. As if a human were not a human. For instance.

A world has come into the world within the world. A compressed world, a petrified perspective, an impassable set meaning, so well-supported, with concrete footings, steel girders, massive welded blocks, colossi, fixed in a dazzling delusion of overdone expression, has come into the world, worked itself out set itself up taken place, a city. A standardized chaos, with the fiction in order.

In a way the city is a mass. A porous mass. A lump with cavities and crevices, with holes, shafts, canals, and tubes, with tunnels, hollows, substrata, introverted chambers. Conjoined containers, tentatively hung up, functioning at last, serving mainly to preserve and snugly enclose the purposely built-in inhabitants. To group them, separate them, give them a place to be while they wait.

In a way the city is a petrification, a hollow arrangement, a calcified land-sponge of concrete, whose labyrinthine branchings and cul-de-sacs force the provisionally present inhabitants to search. This search spreads over networks of roads, buses, trains, via front doors to stairs, elevators, landings, through halls, corridors, at last through front and back rooms to rooms for waiting.

In a way the city is a labyrinth. A labyrinth of lesser labyrinths whose provisionally mobile inhabitants keep the fiction in order, move in measure, for instance toward factories, appropriately, regularly, bound, for instance maintained in time and space by provisionally present things moving in measure, appropriately, regularly, bound to the fiction maintained by the inhabitants.

In a way the city is a fiction. A system of functions functioning just to function, so something else can function and because something else functions. A system of fictions feigning just to feign, so something else can feign and because something else feigns. The provisionally functioning fiction kept in provisional order by provisionally feigning offices etc., etc. until the fiction functions.

In a way the city is an office: a central administration of tendency, motion, illusion. Random life, random death of random inhabitants registered, analyzed, converted to numbers and graphs, quantitative statistics. On a sufficient foundation of randomness, with a sufficient material accumulation of the life, death of irrational elements, it becomes possible to give the illusion a logical form.

11

In a way the city is a logical form. A production producing a consumption consuming a production etc. A production of the provisionally present inhabitants who consume themselves while producing provisionally present things that they also consume. By means of this double consumption the fiction is kept in order, which then keeps the inhabitants in order so that they can live logically.

In a way the city is a double oblivion. A system of consumption capable of hiding all the hidden passages between life and death. An oblivion that avoids seeing itself as oblivion. An oblivious oblivion, forgotten. Hidden beneath obvious presence, the things present in the provisionally present shops, and the subtle structure of things that organizes the inhabitants' restlessness as rest.

In a way the city is rest and order. All the inhabitants who are present, characterized by motion and restlessness, maintain a stable, restful occupation, with each motion, each individual inhabitant's motion, appropriate to all things present, and each restlessness, each individual inhabitant's restlessness, channeled into a collective production of all things present, maintaining rest and order.

In a way the city is a circle. The provisionally mobile inhabitants set themselves and each other in motion and thereby set the circle in motion. In the interim, while the circle keeps the fiction going, the inhabitants slowly move, stand still in parks, squares, and malls, or sit on benches, in restaurants, in movie theaters, as if it were a matter of freedom. So it is a matter of freedom.

In a way it is a matter of freedom. Of forgetting and being forgotten. Covering random death with random life. Laying out labyrinths that hide the place, the places, where the city in passing relieves itself of the things it has consumed: tentative tendencies, immobile motion, disillusioned illusion. Sufficient amounts of random life to give random death a logical form.

They're distributed in large or small houses, large or small apartments, large or small numbers. For instance, a large number in a small apartment, or vice versa. The distribution is just random.

They wait in the bedroom, living room, entry, kitchen, outhouse; or wait in the dayroom, dining room, fireside room, garden room, den, game room, bathroom, in halls, on verandas, in guest rooms.

They wait in streets, alleys, yards. In cellars, in attics. In sheds, storerooms, *pissoirs.* Or wait in gardens and roof gardens. On patios, sundecks. Sheltered on terraces, by the bar, by the pool.

They wait in high-rises, row houses, tract houses, on new and old blocks, in new and old districts, immovable slums, tenements, dark bungalows. Workers' quarters. Or wait where the villas are.

They wait in movie theaters. They wait in buses and department stores, at expos, sales and advertising demonstrations. Or wait at theatres, receptions, concerts, at royal audiences in evening dress.

They wait in factories full of the dust of cotton, metals, dust of poisons, acids and coal, hidden passages between life and death. Or they wait in meetings full of dust from shiny tables.

They wait in trade organizations, unions. As if it were a matter of an endless distance. It's a matter of an overcrowded point where death works undercover. Or wait in city halls, councils, on boards.

They're distributed in large or small functions of large or small fictive values. For instance in large functions of a small or vanishing fictive value. To keep the social fiction alive.

They function because they function, so someone else can function, because someone else functions. Because fiction functions. Because random life, random death, gains meaning from the social fiction.

They feign because they're feigning a society, because they're not alone in feigning, and with their random lives all that's at stake, they want to keep their random deaths out of the fictive form.

They feign because they're feigning a freedom, because they're forced to want to think they're free, and because, thinking they're free, they forget what freedom is, forget their own random death.

They feign because they're feigning an order. Keeping life in order, they think they can keep death in order. They organize life, standardize chaos, and all the while death is organizing everything.

They feign. As if there were something to get away from. As if death in chemical sleep oblivion hushed were something else, as if a human were not a human. And life not a function. Of death.

They feign. As if there were something to look forward to. As if life were not an ever deepening chemical sleep oblivion hushed or a human not a human, loosely flung off hurtling into formlessness.

They feign because they're feigning a life. Feign as freely as only a conflict feigns its stable model. As sensitively as only a life feigns its length, its solitary movements. Its mortality.

They're distributed in lives of varying lengths. Placed in provisional states of varying lengths. States whose lengths they do not know, for whose abrupt ends they wait constantly wait.

They wait in incubators, beds, baby carriages, nurseries, orphanages, preschools. In schools, jails, homes, reception centers. Institutions for wayward youths, disturbed adolescents, and higher education.

They wait in gymnasiums, riding schools, public pools. Wait in cars and ambulances, emergency rooms. Wait and wait in operating rooms and on respirators, in a deeper chemical sleep oblivion hushed.

They wait in barracks for draftees and conscientious objectors, contagious illness and poverty. In control towers, on permanent commissions, in supersonic transports. On security councils. Launch pads.

They wait in camps for refugees, volunteers, soldiers. Centers for rehabilitation, welfare, culture. In secretariats, administrations, ministries, on committees. In ad agencies. Newspaper syndicates.

They wait in hospitals, adult schools, nursing homes. In clinics for X-rays, medicine, artificial organs. Wait in homes for the aged, in various wards for senility, breathing problems, cancer.

They wait in places where they live while they wait. Wait to live while they wait. Live to live. While they wait. Live to live. While they live. While they wait. While they live. Wait. Live.

They're in touch with each other and so can't avoid, say, devouring each other, so they can feed on each other for the rest of their lives.

First of all they kill off parts of themselves, to guarantee that all the remaining parts, though few, can be preserved and perhaps used.

They gain their own inertia, lose their tendency toward free combination with others, because they must deal with others' inertia.

Or they try to alter each other's character and needs, for instance to avoid altering their own character, downgrading their own needs.

They catch each other in a provisional game, reduce each other's lives to restrained details of a life with only random expression.

They function perfectly but without tension or power, without bringing their separate parts, their rules, into play to love each other.

They're absorbed in their parts, shutting out emptiness, and relate freely to each other, especially by being alien to each other.

Meanwhile while they still have excess enough to dole out death so slowly that it looks like life they try to love each other's hatred.

They find a place in the world and hesitate in another world, find the exact place, say, where they hesitate to find each other.

They plumb each other's surfaces, grow mute in each other's sounds, function as each other's death, in a restless world of anaesthesia.

They mingle with each other, plunge, sink into each other, overflow into each other, but they do not burn; they are too mortal for that.

They've come to stay in each other, for as long as it lasts and in order to attain final placement in each other, preferably for life.

They've stiffened in each other, arranged themselves with each other, got each other's situations under control, their fictions in order.

They've laid out layers of impassable permanent meanings in each other to attain immovable significance for each other at last.

They wear each other's masks to play each other's parts, their double games, to the end, at last kill themselves by killing each other.

And they can set aside each other's masks and repeat: life is death. Life might as well get started. Laying out its death to repeat life.

After they've pursued and found each other, stood up for each other, say, for each other's murder of each other, they proliferate.

After keeping each other's lives in form by proliferating, they begin to keep each other's deaths formless and to experiment.

They experiment with each other's freedom, start by talking about each other's freedom until they're tentatively pretending it exists.

They experiment with each other's conflicts, shared conflicts, and formulate all of each other's conflicts in shared stable models.

They experiment with each other's formulations, say, each other's formulations of the length of life and possible future prospects.

They experiment with boundaries between each other, between motion and isolated rest, life they invest and death they get in return.

They experiment with each other's functions, each other's organs, systems, tissues, and skeletons, polish each other's human routines.

They experiment with each other's attempts to outlive each other, to outdistance each other's mortal danger, budding formlessness.

They experiment with each other's non-life as if it were not death, and they exist, say, as humans, as if they were not humans.

They exist as a world in each other's world and serve especially to preserve each other, preserve one dazzled delusion inside the other.

They exist as labyrinths inside each other's labyrinths, whose interminable movements they follow as if following set systems.

They exist as each other's fictions, as images heaped up in each other's illusions, but pretend it's a matter of logical forms.

They pretend their stable production of each other's consumption is on a par with their own deepest urges to consume each other.

They pretend it's possible to forget each other's random death in a world where presence, motion, illusion, create their own world.

They pretend their random life is not a function of death, loosely flung off, already formless, but in another world.

They pretend life is not a steadily deepening chemical sleep oblivion hushed increasingly slow anaesthesia fall vanishing. Nothing.

They pretend they're waiting to live, to make it possible for someone to live, tentatively as if asleep, pretend to live.

Someone walks into a house and looks at the street from his window.

Someone walks out of a house and looks at his window from the street.

Someone walks down a street and looks at the others on his way.

Someone walks in on his way and looks at a house as his own.

Someone is always on his way and never notices houses.

Someone never notices the others walking down the street.

Someone always notices himself when he goes out for a walk.

Someone goes for walks in the street in order to notice himself.

Someone notices himself and walks into others' houses.

Someone comes out of others' houses but doesn't look at them.

Someone comes back to his own house but doesn't turn on the light.

Someone doesn't want to be looked at and sits alone in the dark.

Someone walks around in the dark looking for light in a house.

Someone has lights in his house but doesn't expect anyone to come.

Someone always expects somebody but forgot to turn on the light.

Someone expects somebody to come show him into the house.

Someone shows somebody that the house has vanished among the others.

Someone shows somebody that the house can't be the right house.

Someone turned out the light in the right house and went away.

Someone went for a walk in order not to show anyone the wrong house.

Someone went away because he looked at the house in the wrong way.

Someone went the wrong way because he saw light in a house.

Someone went the right way when somebody showed him the wrong way.

Someone showed somebody the wrong way and went to turn the light on.

Someone turns on the light in the right house but doesn't see it.

Someone is blind and doesn't need the right house at all.

Someone does need a house but isn't blind enough.

Someone needs somebody else enough to be blind.

Someone shows somebody the way though he's never seen him before.

Someone has vanished because he was shown the right way.

Someone has vanished from somebody he usually walks with.

Someone walks with somebody he usually doesn't need.

Someone is blind to somebody who usually wants to walk with him.

Someone is pursued by somebody who otherwise would have vanished.

Someone is so hotly pursued that he vanishes into the house.

Someone vanished in the house and would hardly walk to the window.

Someone vanished in another house that is otherwise deserted.

Someone vanished in the street and shows himself to no one.

Someone has been abandoned and comes out only when darkness falls.

Someone abandons his house and never returns to it.

Someone breaks into a house and lives there as long as possible.

Someone lives in a house that is otherwise abandoned day and night.

Someone lives in a house whose windows don't face the street.

Someone lives in a house without windows and has stopped seeing.

Someone lives in a house without light and never looks at himself.

Someone has stopped expecting anyone and never comes out.

Someone has stopped looking at the light and is blind at last.

Someone has stopped showing how alone he is in the dark.

Someone has vanished in his house and has never seen himself.

Someone is alone in his house and never needs the others.

Someone has vanished among the others and hasn't been seen since.

Someone is alone with himself and has never known the others.

Someone is alone with the others and has never known himself.

Someone is alone because he's been unable to imagine anything else.

Someone is alone because he has been able to imagine something else.

Someone is alone because he's vanished into his thoughts.

Someone is always alone and looks at himself as dying.

Someone is lying dead in a house whose windows face the street.

Someone is lying dead in a house whose lights are all on.

Someone is dead in a house that is otherwise completely abandoned.

Someone is dead where no one ever expected to find anyone.

Someone is dead and suddenly shows up among all the others.

Someone is dead and is looked at by those walking by anyway.

Someone is dead and is carried out of his house as darkness falls.

Someone is dead and is looked at by someone who is blind at last.

Someone stands still and is alone at last with the other dead person.

LOGOS

1

Desolation without anyone ever having been there,
            having died, and then not being there;
without there being either a definite
            or a random place,
                  not random because it
                        lacks placelessness,
                  not definite because it
                        is placeless,
                  without definition, random or not.
Like pure being where there is nothing.

Outside: all the dirt
            hurry death destruction words
            juices beginnings confusion: inside.

2

Darkness: a missing sun here and there,
stars that normally, if they could
normally be seen, could disclose a mortal
gathering, almost an environment, far off.

Or light: a warning light buzzes
but no one calls out, reacts:
the explosion gains speed and the darkness
hides what might have happened

3

In the background: stones, cliffs,
mountains sawn from plywood, painted,
drawn from someone's
memory of some drawing
of rugged peaks.

In the foreground: no one can remember
what, if the background were not
as described, described
an abrupt movement toward everything:
the undescribed.

To the right: a little moss, a solitary
plant: plastic and batting.
To the left: beings, milling around
if the current is turned on.

In addition plans for an artificial
rain that will of course awaken
a completely indescribable longing.

4

When and if the sets burn,
when and if a figure clings
        in fear to these set pieces
when and if this figure even
           perseveringly utters screams
                for instance for help,
when and if this happens it will be understood:

that the man working the spotlight
obviously knows what he is doing,
that he has obviously just waited
until the time was ripe.

5

In front of the mountains, and before the mountains
burn or break up as planned,
houses are set up, but just houses
that are not real houses, but just real
fronts of unreal houses
into which everyone can easily run
when the artificial rain begins

6

Everything is put in place and taken away:

oceans are filled in with countries
rivers are filled in with roads
lakes are filled in with islands
excess ice masses,
hidden springs and groundwater,
water in sewers, oases,
raindrops, dew, all are gathered,
poured into volcanoes, and evaporate;

abysses are filled in with mountains,
subways with buildings,
houses with still more houses,
cities with cities, all with all,
till everything is full,
till everything is whole, without division,
impossible to divide
and with no correlates in language.

Everything can thereupon and therefore be taken away
and put in some completely different place.

7

After the stage, having been
painstakingly rinsed with acid,
corroded and vanished, the stench
came, nausea, hollowness,
the words' craving for sets:

"mirror" wanted a mirror,
"belch" wanted a belch,
even "acid" wanted some acid,
"set" a set;
the words
created their own states of being,
made a world out of "world."

8

Time: dregs of words
            like nubbly slugs.

Place: solidarity of things
             like random stones.

Motion: slime-tracks
               of slugs on stones

Delusion: all metaphors'
                 theories of unity.

1

A word flies up   tentatively   Flocks hap-
hazardly follow   Firm biological forms As
if it were a matter of confidence It is
a matter of an outermost boundary   desolation/non-desolation:

a word that flies up   flocks that fol-
low   neither more nor less   birds that
fill this endlessly vanishing space
with a lack of explanation

It is a matter of the very vaguest explan-
ation Maintain this explanation to the end
Turn on the wind machine and let angels with
beating wings be moved sovereign as satellites

Let fleets of oddly backward creatures hurtle
away on the wind   let insects with sails
huge and stripped as shining illusions stand
as a vision: the resistance of being to purity

2

They are strangely constructed, the shadows of words;
from inside the darkness they see light as dark;
they fetter the sources of words to their murder
and draw on the language's inherent drought.

It is words that incessantly bear a dead paradox
dying incessantly, visions unborn,
like stars that are finally burned down to carbon
or lightning itself struck by lightning in storms.

It is shadows arising near word walls of logic
biological forms, spread as they decompose
revealing a madness that underlies language
razed gardens behind iron fencing that grows

It is strangely the words hide their own propaganda
a trust in exactly the stuff of their faults
a landslide turned inward, a muted mutation
a wounded milieu wherein suffering exults.

3

A gray misty morning over the painted mountains
Whether the birds will waken is still uncertain
Memory
A stone rolling down from the mountains

On a solitary plant a leaf moves
In a mossy hollow the pale stalks stir
A breeze
Whether the sound will carry is still uncertain

No one is there yet
No one is there to hear and see
Hesitation
A state of being, waiting for a word

The painted mountains vanish
Plants and moss are enfolded in earth
The mist vanishes
A stone flies up over the mountains

4

When the finishing touches have been put on
the mountains When the stars have finally
been plugged in(to) When the sun is put
in place And when the spacing of everything

has been re-established When the rain is dammed up
in the floating tanks When the white balloon-
clouds are released at last And when buoy-
ancy and weight are successfully wrestled into

balance When the sap has finally been pumped
into every single plastic leaf And
when the collective programming of the mobile
creatures has mapped out the only

possible courses When the performers have finally
been taught their places and the man who
works the spotlight replaced with a com-
puter The whole staff will talk about fate

5

It was to be like feelings
It was to be like the summer destroyed
It was to be like the cool pause
                    in the middle of a word

It was to be like feelings
It was to be like a blow a lapse
It was to be like the sweet lapse of forms
                    into formlessness

It was to be like feelings
It was to be like a denser formlessness
It was to be like a boisterous confidence
                    in biology

It was to be like feelings
It was to be like an eternal interim
It was to be like being
                    It was what it was

6

When the diagram of the stage is tied in
        with the diagram of what is off stage
When the word is tied down to the thing
        and objectively determined by the state of things

When language has at last settled out
        say, along the lines of the oldest minerals
and when style has clearly settled in
        say, along the lines of transparent crystals

When communication
        (say, along the lines of the words used:
        tied in tied down settled out settled in)
is settled, tied, and trapped

then choice dream and history must
        (say, along the lines of the obscurest utopias)
write themselves between the lines
        (say, along the lines of the youngest guerilla)

7

Because it will end in unbearable scenes
Because the conditions for doing things for others are others
Because the corpses were doused with acid long ago
Because the stench stimulates sociability

Because the void (say, in the stomach) stimulates production
Because nausea creates fertile ground for artificial needs
Because acid triggers the craving for fullness
Because the belch is part of politics

Because the conditions for belching are reserved for the few
Because a place in the wings is reserved for the few
Because things happen in the wings
Because these things must not come to light

Because words set the stage for the world
Because the world keeps words in their places
Because there exists a loathing for it all
        the mirror has a kind of inverted validity
                    that the truth lacks

8

The change desired is never exactly like
                              the change attained
The change attained has nothing in common with
                              the actual change
The actual change is deprived of its actuality by
                              psychic dislocations
The psychic dislocations are permanently unknown

    In practice unity will be proven impossible
    Time place motion no
    they will never merge here

It's a matter of indeterminate points
    (dream/infinitely receding image/bio-
    logical signal)
    where language and the world brush inform de-
    form or whatever each other

    so that the world continues just continues
    in spite of the will to change
    which continues just continues

    In practice it will be possible to create solidarity
        through long-term physical contact

    In practice it will be possible to destroy solidarity
        through short-term psychic contact

    In practice what happens/has happened will
        stay unformulated

1

A garden a stair an image a direction
Air
    (Air slipping away from the speak-
    ers so words never proliferate
    but settle like rime on
    their lips)

A stair leading into an image
An image at the end of a garden
Flowers
        (Flowers that are never named
        because the words never proliferate/
        the words that never flower)

An image of a garden
        (An image slipping away from
        the speakers)

An image of a garden at the end of an image
of a garden
        (An image slipping away with
        the speakers)

A direction (thick with frost)

A stair (leading at last into the ruined
        lips of the speakers/the angels)

2

Beneath these blankets of snow/these dregs
of sun: the eye of the storm completely
still in the heart   in the heart? no one is
there yet   but in the chaos of the
cells/within their aimless tumbling/
"thoughtlessnesses" there is a
confidence in everything random: inter-
vention "proclamations" small explosions or
"insanity" gatherings fetters fences

Beneath these layers of garden painted from
garden to garden, beneath these sha-
dows stretching from image
to image/from the bush in one
over the path in the other the mountain
in the third   and farther on over
the same endless expanse covered
with snow   with white-painted snow

Beneath these continuous continuations

3

The painted surface splits
the varnish blisters   peels
and the base coat matte white
dissolves   vanishes   some day
                      like melting snow
the world ends there

And there it begins   gratuitously
its life/death a matter of course, period

The birds waken/The murder takes place

4

A fire alarm rings deep inside the fire

The possible courses were possible only before

Even a sun disintegrates now and then

Only strangely/clearly do you hear
                              the aesthetic echo of death
                                        ("fate")

5

the world as thought as dreamed
       (as in a longing to dissolve)
      as seen as carried out
      (as new growth in what is destroyed)
      as put in place
      (as foam after the fire)
      as subordinate to the image
            (the will of the image)
      (as fire put out with white-painted snow)
      as a set

the set as thought as dreamed
      (as a confidence in longing)
      as seen as carried out
      (as in a countermove to longing)
      as put in place
      (as the possibility of fire)
      as subordinate to the image
            (the will of the image)
      (as snow that melts meeting fire)
      as the world

6

When it's all white on white
When the diagram of the stage/the stage/and the world
     (give way and vanish in a fog)
      are painted white
When the distinction between inside and outside/the
       osmotic pressure between the image
       of the world and the world vanishes
      (and only the loathing and apathy are left)
      and only the membrane white and use-
      less   limp is left
When the white paint   is not paint   is
      not white   and is not any-
      thing else
     (and everything is withheld from the senses/from language)
      then it's all over, immaterially ended
      and the world slowly returns

7

There are war scenes on tapestries hung
along the whole Maginot Line

meticulous prints of the Spanish Armada
afloat on the seas of the world

While Potemkin on the front page of *Izvestia*
is shipwrecked on a Pacific island

Or statues: Ivan the Terrible
smiles at the sight of Harlem

de Gaulle rides into Wenceslas Square
at the head of the Red Armies

and huge modern sculptures: the Great Wall of China
between Spain and Spain

While Napoleon dies on Formosa

8

That's the way the world is
short on truth

the principal parties
cover a dreaming market
with dreams

with luxury tactics/
                    /time must not go to waste

That's why the tables are important
a collection of static tables
in a collection of static strategic places
(fantastic genre paintings/
at the foot of a mountain   in a marsh on a beach
in streets in forests everywhere that there's room
for a table a table is set up a table where all
possible parties can buy each other a round)
The goal is actually to glut the world with tables

. . . si l' Être est caché,
cela même est un trait de l' Être
M. Merleau-Ponti

1

Bit by bit as the stage is described
it gets more and more obvious that
it's not described but concealed
For instance the word desolation is
in itself a denial of itself
(of itself a denial in itself)
And when it's said that words fly
(like birds that fill an end-
lessly vanishing space)
it's probably to conceal the fact
that the words are not one
with the world they describe.
Words do not have wings.
And they neither flower nor will
but they take potential flowers
and set them in a garden
which they then set
in an image of a garden
which they then set
in an image, etc.
The words stay where they are
while the world vanishes
This is a criticism of the way language is used
Because it's a criticism of the way things are.

Avec comme pour langage
rien qu'un battement aux cieux
Stéphane Mallarmé

2

What's written is always something else
And what's described is something else again
Between them lies the undescribed
which as soon as it's described
opens up new undescribed areas
It's indescribable
Even though darkness is defined by light
and light by darkness
something's always left out.
And even if this something is "defined"
as razed gardens
behind iron fencing that grows
the logic is always left
And even though the logic is not defined
but concealed beneath layers of gardens
painted from garden to garden
there's still a restlessness left
a despair
a pulse with no body
This is a criticism of the body
because it's a criticism of life.

. . . l'horreur liée à la vie
comme un arbre à la lumière
Georges Bataille

3

In light of the impossible relationship
that exists between nothing and everything
or just between nothing and something
even between nothing and the word nothing
and because of the complete silence of language
about everything that doesn't happen
either in the world or not in the world
this stance ought to be abandoned.
It's abandoned and leaves behind
either a language that's a result of the world
or a world that's a result of language
either a sky seas and mountains
or painted skies seas and mountains
either birds that waken/murder that takes place
or stones that fly up over mountains
it's hopeless
it's impossible
In light of this impossible relationship
that exists between either and or
or just between either and both
even between either and the word either
and because of the complete silence of language
about everything that doesn't happen
either in either or not in either
this stance ought to be adopted
Now we're back where we started!
This is a criticism of fiction
because it's a criticism of our longing for the world

vous êtes déjà mortes au monde
Sade

4

"I" do not want any more sets
"I" do not want any more anecdotes
            about painted mountains
"I" do not want to see any more universes appear
            within the bounds of reason
"I" do not want to hear any more fire alarms ring
            every time the sun rises
"I" do not want to vanish
"I" am the one who has written the above
            and the one writing the following
"I" will not pretend that I am dead
I am afraid
This is a criticism of every "poetics"
because it's a criticism of the fear of true powerlessness

les causes sont peut-être
inutiles aux effets
Sade

5

I've tried to tell about a world that doesn't exist
in order to make it exist. The air hanging motionless
in the air above the fields outside the city where I
no longer go. The joy of a familiar distance. The peace
of a familiar restlessness. As during high fevers, the
delight of meaning nothing.

I've tried to keep the world at a distance. It's been easy.
I'm used to keeping the world at a distance. I'm alien.
I'm most comfortable being alien. That way I forget the
world. That way I stop crying and raging. That way the world
becomes white and inconsequential.

And I wander where I will. And I stand completely still.
That way I get used to being dead.

This is a criticism of the power human beings have over language
because it's a criticism of the power language has over human beings.

Le monde ne peut être dit "hu-
main" que dans la mesure où il
signifie quelque chose
                                            A.-J. Greimas

6

It's first and foremost to me that the world
means something
I assume that there are others to whom the world
means something
It's first and foremost to them that the world
means something
Anyone could have written this
So it surprises me that others
experience something similar
that meanings I assign to the world here
are assigned by others to the world here and there
in a similar way
that from the manifold meanings
such a uniform ambiguity arises
that even the world is the same
Even the world that has no secrets
before I get into it
Even the world that has no truth
before I get into it
Even the world inside me as
the matter we share with each other
even the world is the same
same old matter
that we share with each other:

in itself of itself for itself
without meaning
but outside itself
here for instance where I appear
as someone writing about the world
here and there for instance where somebody appears
as someone reading about the world
here and there and everywhere the world is
something else and more than it is
like a meaningful disagreement between us

Vieil océan, ô grand célibataire
quand tu parcours la solitude
solonnelle de tes royaumes fleg-
matiques . . . .

Lautréamont

7

It's not so easy to get around this kind of thing
It's not that there's any perspective on the world
It's not that there's any overview of the world
It's not that there's any understanding of the world
It's that there's not any understanding of the world
It's that the world is incomprehensible immaterial on the outside
while I'm alone
I critique myself
I deal with myself
as a disagreement between myself
and a world that's incomprehensible immaterial on the outside
I myself am incomprehensible immaterial on the outside
but not on the inside
I'm not that way when I'm alone
just between us, I'm not that way here now
when you read
that I write
that I'm not that way
and when you read
that I write
that you're not that way
On the contrary
You're an old ocean yourself
You're a phlegmatic kingdom yourself
You traverse your own solemn loneliness
It's not the ocean that becomes comprehensible

It's not the kingdom that becomes material
It's not the loneliness that comes inside
It's you It's me It's the disagreements between us
This in itself is the image of a political poem.

. . . la pleine réalité: J'imagine
le début d'un livre . . .

Philippe Sollers

8

Happiness is the change that comes over me
when I describe the world
It comes over the world
Happiness is the change that comes over me
when I'm afraid
It comes over the world
For instance I can be afraid of and for the world
afraid because the world consists among other things
of me so swiftly dying
Happiness is this change
happiness is that it comes over me
this disintegration slow sorrow
this security
within it I'm completely restless
within it I'm completely immeasurably mute
within it I'm deaf blind and stupid without feeling
Within it I start to spin fables about the world

1

My world is clear I sleep I lie in my enclosure
here in my assigned place between feet hair and darkness
assigned to sleep and phases of identity. I am an object.

They say that in bed you learn to die.

Remembering that after a while the blood will rerun the usual
images   aimlessly
and that I if it's me will find aims in this chemistry

They say that in bed you learn to shut up

Learn to confide in the meaningless dreams

Learn that in a way it's possible to live
an exclusive death

That's the only way I'm meaningless enough
That's the only way I'm humanly possible

wrongly placed as I am in a right world
rightly placed as I am in a wrong world

placed   world

learn all this that I won't need tomorrow
tomorrow when I wake if I wake
and the dream comes singing toward me
we want the world and we want it now

2

I talk about the world, meaning Nature as such from
                    first to last cultural nature

I talk about the world, meaning my own private and
                    fleeting unknown portion of the monstrous mass

I talk about the world, meaning a society
                    not a society   not associated
                    meaning an action
                    not just one action but many

Talk about an interaction

Talk about intercessions
            interventions
            interruptions
                    mean so well So what exactly is
                                wrong
                Why do these words mean that there is
                                something wrong
                                    Is there always
                                something wrong
                                something between two
                                    among many
                                    among us all

Does no interstice exist
            that's not an empty zone
            and not a battle zone

                    just a play of lines
                              intermediate shadows
                                        positions
                                        things
                    an interregnum
                              where we all can go
                                             lie down
                                        and be
                              outside ourselves
                    joined in comprehension of the joint incomprehensibility

I'm talking about the inchoate forms of communication
                    the interfaces of thought
              talking about the interbeddings of feelings
              Why shouldn't that be the only world

3

The only world is the only one to us
The only world is indescribable to us
It writes itself
   as if you imagined the air over the earth
   as breaths rising from millions of mouths
   as breaths as words as cries   as chemical com-
   binations of the terror of life and the
   terror of losing it
   this air is our lone indecipherable writing
   this air is our joint incomprehensible creation condition

   a sign a tremor clouds frost
   and we answer with storms tears evaporations

   along the way we make measurements charts statistics
   along the way we make notes on each other's notes
   as the writing vanishes
   as it rains as we write about the snow
   as it snows as we write about the sun
   as we cry as we laugh as we write about the first
   time we cried laughed etc. etc.

As the words storm away through the world
As I catch one here one there
inevitably randomly   the only thing   to do
describe one confusion against the other with the other
as the sky is completely clear

4

It's all something I've borrowed from the world
I use it as I please and say in a fit
   of bravery what you own is your own and it's mine
   have even heard myself in a fit of rashness
   you're safe with your own that's the kind of thing you say
For instance I've borrowed every word up to now and now and
   I'm blithely borrowing more
and I've borrowed what I've thought
   what I think while I write
   while I wrote
For instance I've borrowed this sentence: I am dead
   It's not a pronouncement
      not a confession
      not a meaningless plea/assertion
   it's something I got from the world
   it's with that kind of sentence that the world
   keeps me on my toes
   it's with that kind of sentence that the world
   creates its image of me

Better this than a speech about responsibility and powerlessness

5

My world is discontinuous
            in relation to the world as a whole
            and in relation to you
            it has wings
My world is a language through water
            with the shining nerves distributed
            as when the sun in water randomly generously
            anyway it has wings

            Wings of water

And I want you to know that it has a certain effect
        it has a certain tingly effect
        a rejoicing at the absence of cause
        Leap says the world and I fly

That's how I drown my world in the world

6

In May the lilacs will bloom; they must!
All the earth's resources rushing
    Between sky and streets
    What a relief!

    No more timeless creations conditions
    But the energies the conflicts of the world
    as coming possibilities Summers

    This white ecstasy

    It means alert
    It means poised
        like moist lips on the way to the kiss
    It means that the kiss
        and the sound of the kiss electronically amplified
                sound like lilacs
                this rushing sound of carbonation
                these fizzing stillnesses
                loving
Yes here the world means lilacs
    means nothing else   nothing else but lilacs
    but the fact that it means anything at all
                makes it almost human

7

To assault loneliness
    whip up seas and tear seeds away
    from becalmed plants
    drive words out of overfed brains
    they're too well-off
    they're like eggs   their paralysis is social

To march myself out through the window
    aim straight into your heart
    fill it with opium sugar and blindness
    fill it with violent cries
      as when love is recognized
      as when the poetry of habit is compromised
      as when the world is extravagant

I'm thinking of the global implications
I'm thinking of the dialectics of liberation
I'm thinking of the supreme disorder of the vision

I cannot see that you are not me

8

There the full reality
There imagination beginning and the full reality
There transferable impressions trance/consciousness
        this *go* from world to world
        this pulse

        this nuisance/essence that makes the world insane
        and reveals the identical person

During sex beauty is sure of itself
During sex the body is alone
                        asyntactic
                        schizophrenic in its happiness
During sex the world is a caress

It's the whole thing
It has no poetry in it
It's not even comprehensible

1

Erupting like swellings
obscene sexual ploys
strikes blockades and power struggles sweetness/
let this be a first inaccessible phase
let this be detached facts and stimuli delusion
it's seen from inside
there's nowhere else to see it from
it's the same for everyone
so these three synonyms must come into play:
        traumatic chemistry
        political consciousness
        internal sexuality of words

when they built the city it was spring and no one noticed
      the shadows
when they built the shadows they felt at home/they bathed
      and slept together
and they rubbed their skin hard and the wind blew the remnants
      away
and they lay down in the beds under the city and forgot
      everything

that's the way they report each ritual
that's the way they report brightly to themselves as to mirrors
that's the way they see only what they understand
in a way they understand everything

But as the pain and swelling spread settle re-
    flecting themselves
    (as political speakers' sex organs set in plaster)
and as the walls grow by themselves/act by themselves
    masturbate copulate with themselves
    (as gestures and deeds/words deported from the politi-
    cians' bodies)
the negative reports are strengthened and aggravated
    a crack in the wall begins to sing
    a rumor forged onto a doorframe rattles in the wind
    stomachs distended between houses rumble impatiently
this is a second inaccessible phase
these are the earsplitting utopian facts

We creep on like ants without ears with our beautiful mat-
    ter on our backs
our function is to be incomprehensible
our function is to be
our function

2

To gather the sunlight-clear details into a god of semen
to enamel hopeless words with secretions
to move in blue opalescent bodies
as in the city that flows in the blood
as in the blood that flows in the city
in pleasure
senses
metabolism
to feel that an arm is a street/stop/that a head is a mall in
a suburb/stop/that a breast is a brownstone in Brooklyn/stop/
the stomach a factory in Yokohama/stop/the bowels a tree/stop/
in a back yard in Frankfurt/stop/intercourse/stop/a Concorde
landing in Tivoli Gardens/stop/to send this message/stop/for
your sake/stop/to fill this endlessly vanishing city/stop/with
a lack of explanation/stop/for your sake/stop/for your sake for
your sake we are all metaphors for each other

3

Turning to new ways to live out a passion
Going out to find the nearest tree and describe it
Finding a tree at any rate And describing it
Throwing the description away Going home
Sitting very still in a chair and having an orgasm

4

I've now looked at trees from above
                              from the side
                              and from below
I've even been up in a tree
            and looked at other trees
              looked at light
              seen it turn green
as if a human were not a human
but a leaf a branch   entropy

In spite of that, I create, in the dark
                              on the way home
                              inside myself
              images chills frosts
              fictive trees dead in the world
              difficult and blue
as if nature had leaped into death
                              in me
(and nature actually does make leaps)

5

Leap says the world
          and the world stands perfectly still
houses streets cars with people
                              perfectly still
They drive out and look at a tree

I find it strange that I can never tell them
          something they haven't seen

6

It's in this city (forest language)
                    that we share with each other
or in the city that we dream I dream
                    when I'm removed and put in a completely
                                                    different place
                    (it's the city that's put in a completely
                                                    different place)
it's in this removed city that never comes closer
it's there that I am
        there that I go around like a magnet
                                a principle
                    suck in coincidences
                    spit them out as systems
                                hey, world!

7

Beloved world
      that functions as an image of the world
Beloved image
      that functions as a change in the world
Beloved constancy
      that functions as a source of confusion
Our life together
      is a sexual and therefore mental
or is a mental and therefore sexual
                              activity   my love!

8

There the full reality
       I think what I see with my eyes
       I see with my eyes what I think

There the full reality
       they think what they see with their eyes
       they see with their eyes what they think

There the full reality   the intrigue
       they think what I see with my eyes
       they see with their eyes what I think

     the urge to break free
           get perspective
           create order
   the urge for a stronger stimulus

     zero loathing   zero world   zero me
   let this be a third inaccessible phase
   orgasm as convulsion and absence—hey, clown!

1

points flowers circles flowers ellipses flowers radii
flowers tangents flowers quadrants flowers lines flow-
ers etc. flowers

birds with clipped wings beak to tail com-
      pletely still
      keep mincing along the tangent   It
      has begun

      in the center the rosette of wings   It was there
      that it began   Begins

designed like a garden   but with no entrances
      paths or exits

possible interpretation: a mirror
                        for what can't be seen

2

a pulse with no body a sun with no sky
a gathering warmth that beats in the sand
blood that consistently drives up the fever
in houses whose pipes should have water instead

a fever that worships its own fever-nature
and moves itself outside where everything stays
where snow with its striking and subzero culture
burns into the body like rags set ablaze

a grief with no luxury a pillar with no base
a body that's lost the code of its entrails
a shred of a brain an unusual clutter
telegrams missing the planet by miles

3

in labyrinths of light and light-green leaves
in terror-labyrinths where the sky is clear
                              and life a matter of course
                                    far too matter-of-course
there is a taste of plaster of stone of crowbar

off-limits   no entry   danger

I am a face that turns its face away
        a stone that when it turns over
                              is a stone

4

I borrowed a tear from the water
And wept it again and again
A fool I had known from the country
That doesn't exist was my friend

I heard him incessantly saying
That foolishness must be maintained
Then we praised the water that weeps
And the fool who knows where he steps

5

watersteps stoneskies windhouses
aircellars rainhearts sandbodies
cliffmouths riverstomachs icesexes
snowlungs coalbrains cloudfingers
saltnerves eartheyes heartache

6

a black storm in a sealed cave
black lilacs smelling of sulfur
black snow

conversations with death:
freedom freedom freedom

the snow falls
piles itself in great drifts on the sky
and the sky is completely black

In May the lilacs will bloom; they must!

7

In another atmosphere in trembling joy in unthinkable things that are
thought anyway
imagination like sugar-scum   what we call horrors on the edge of
joy
on the edge where a bird sits
it drinks nothing
it sings of nothing
in this way the magic generates its signs of life
the birds fall
and in quantities of light-years we see their death

8

Inside the first fable there is a second, inside the second there is
a third, inside the third there is a fourth fable etc.

Inside fable no. 3517 a man sits telling about a
greenhouse inside the greenhouse there was a garden inside the garden there was a
greenhouse inside the greenhouse . . . . .

in garden no. 1423 a man sits telling about a garden
where a man sits telling about a garden where
a man sits . . . . .

man no. 8611 tells a long string of fables

inside fable no. 4280 a man has been sitting and waiting all this
time I go up to him My name is _____ he says Then he tells
me a little about himself

1

If the stage revolves I'll consider it a plus
there's no reason to mention fate it's crude
I mean there's no reason to look at an owl
as if swallows, lapwings, etc. didn't exist
remembering how they flapped around on their own
in flocks that were never part of the picture
Come to think of it the owls were never part of the picture either
typically enough: most things are hidden

Paradise wasn't part of it either   A garden
I saw in a picture once and one
I once was in were both part of it
it was purely by chance   typically enough
chance is the only thing that really expresses
the longing for Paradise   The longing was part of it
because the truth was never part of it
because the truth is never part of it

2

It rains The sun shines It snows
There are storms The weather is quite varied
Depending on the various areas of the earth
The earth spins And some day it will vanish
Like sand vanishing between fingers
Without any fingers existing
It will just vanish And the sand will vanish
And the image of the earth as sand that will vanish will vanish

But for now the earth is still spinning
And is quite different from sand vanishing
Is big and solid and has room for a lot of people
In a lot of varied areas
Where the weather is quite varied
It snows for instance or it rains or there are storms
The sun shines Or the moon and stars shine
Love Love Love Happy happy love

3

I see that a cat lies sunning itself
It lies in a space between buildings It licks its paws
For the most part it is still The space is empty
But an empty orange juice can lies there too
A plant grows up through a crack
The shadow of the plant moves
I do not know it It is green
The space must have been meant for something

Behind the space there is a wall
It must be a house
It must be the back of a house
The house must have a front
It must have windows there
After all it is in the middle of the city
The city has spread amazingly
And it spreads more and more

4

If I write that the tree stands on a plain
Perhaps that it stands in a field Alone
That the leaves are gray that the trunk is hollow
That the crown is a violent and burning red
That it is therefore a hawthorn That the crown is green
That the leaves wither That the flowers are scented
That the tree functions In order to function
I have done what I could to see

The time it has taken for the tree to die
And the time it has taken for me
Enter into simple chemical combination
Space visions dreams facts
Space in which I stand on a plain Alone
Visions in which the tree looks at my leaves
Dreams in which the body is hollow the skull blooms
Facts in which time is palpable space

5

Houses with broad imposing stairs
Doors with brass knobs Polished
Cool corridors with whitewash and tile
Rooms with chairs tables beds
Improvised electrical wiring
Septic tanks for wastes
Water for poisons
Light for eyes

It's not at all a matter of adjustment
Not at all a matter of survival
More or less would do
It's a matter of everything
Which can be the least thing in the world
Or something in motion in the world
Or the world in motion in me
Formulate Formulate Formulate

6

While the water runs from the higher points on down
While the water is forced up through the pipes in the houses
While the snow melts on the mountainsides
While the ice is frozen in lockers
While the sun burns
While the rooms in the houses are kept temperate
While the birds sing
While the newspapers come out

While the mountains slowly erode
While the buildings squares are decorated
While the trees turn green
While the women give birth
While the flowers wither
While the graves are closed
While the rain falls
While the pulse beats

7

The city is now so big that chance rules
A fusion of art and life
A door leading into a house
And out into a street
A street that leads to a long string of houses
That lead to a long string of streets
Squares where the sky lands
Shocks that proliferate

Names no one can get straight
Streets with forgotten slum clearance projects
Finds from various times
Charts in drawers
Museums with corpses
A stuffed car on a pedestal
Magnets with sores
Love Love Love Happy happy Love

8

A happy machine
A wild imagination
A fantastic din
A wheel standing still
You don't notice it
You run for your life
A word that strikes home
The dogs bark

1

A desert can be so desolate
That no one believes it exists
The dead can be so dead
That no one can see they exist

They just lie around in the sand
Looking like wrack of the sea
They lie there and wait for the water
To come set the process free

2

It's morning, morning and sunrise
In full overpowering light
And even a commonplace body
Can tell it is new after night

It's beginning to sing of the sun
It's important that sun break the wall
It's beginning to shine like the sun
It's important that body is all

3

A stone rolls down from the mountains
Sisyphus pushes it up
A stone rolls down from the mountains
Sisyphus pushes it up

A stone rolls down from the mountains
Sisyphus pushes it up
Sisyphus sings:
A stone flies up over the mountains

4

Upon a strange stone there sits a man
They have grown together—how strange
He says he is drawing a cherry branch
Floating out of the cherry tree's range

So you watch him drawing that cherry branch
Floating out of the cherry tree's range
It resembles a man sitting on a strange stone
They have grown together—how strange

5

And then he steps out of the stone
As if leaving his stony reality
And then he steps onto the stage
A model of split personality

And he dances around on the stone
And tramples it breath by breath
And then he falls dead on the stage
As if dying a natural death

6

And then they step out of language
As if they were made of words
And then they whirl back into language
As if they were made of earth

And then back and forth between vision
And consciousness they fly
Until they're so weakened that life
Strikes like a bolt from the sky

7

And then they are finally there
And then they drink sugar and snow
And some start to weep and to wonder
And some start to laugh and to know

And then with their bodies together
They decide to try out what could be
And some go completely crazy
And some are beginning to see

8

A society can be so stone-hard
That it fuses into a block
A people can be so bone-hard
That life goes into shock

And the heart is all in shadow
And the heart has almost stopped
Till some begin to build
A city as soft as a body

1

There are soldiers positioned in highly improbable places
with tanks camouflaged as giant impregnated stones
The soldiers consider their ration of possible pleasures
but pleasures are often such rapidly mutating genes

They're positioned to further the interests of wealthy cartels
Their deployment bears fruit for the economy of the nation
From the outset the bomb that they drop is an infant deformed
From the outset the bomb is a shattered imagination

And their hour will come as if it had come in a dream
their semen converted to superheated TNT
as if all their thoughts were searing electric currents
and their screams were a copy of sirens that cry

The only thing left: an eternally sorry reunion
with something that never was anything other than killed
The only thing left: engrossing financial interests
for the handful in power to have and to hold

2

Their dealings with suns and with other occasional stars
have taught them to count on the grayish inertia of masses
Their churches are built on the slag heaps of fire-gutted minds
and they fully support any strategy furthering stasis

It's a matter of pudgy small cardinals, easily frightened
who think they can even declare that the sun has turned black
The worst of it is that the louder they clamor
the farther the masses' sun is forced back

It's a matter of cowards who also are wide-awake jackals
They consider the status quo equitable all in all
They swallow the meat for which others have paid with their labors
because those same others have swallowed their theories whole

It's a matter of angels resembling contemptuous condors
who greet everyone with their horribly lovable smiles
In all the world's wrong little offices they have their quarters
while the masses are bent to their idiosyncratic styles

3

There are surpluses ranging from barley to artichokes
going unsold unless profits are good
There are overfed hogs growing heavier daily
as appetite boosters are mixed with their food

There are rice and tomatoes piled sky-high and rotting
and warehouses reeking of moldering meat
There are ministers of agriculture, stern prelates
washing their hands of starvation and need

There is fish to feed everyone, protein aplenty
filling the nets of the starving and then
seized by the pulsating social machinery
that lets just the well fed be fed once again

There are those who have long had a clear understanding
that sharing the profits is wise and is fair
And yet they believe the goodwill of the people
can live upon talk, exploitation, and air

4

Energy is the world's joy radiating
faces are radiant when people feel good
Sorrow the look of those who stand shivering
simply because they must go without food

5

Within the society Mr. Sade sits by the side of the bound girl
He slowly caresses a shoulder a breast
He breathes that the whole can quite easily yield
and the parts' more disjointed desire can come first

Then he rapidly relativizes her parts
and whips them together in his practised way
until the girl looks like an unconceived whole
an impossible thing like a night in broad day

And then he recites from his writings about
society's more metaphysical light
He thinks the entire machine's being run
by the sexual mystique of the struggle for might

But no one dares see a political model
that burns its way down to a young girl's bone
For napalm is merely America's trademark:
You're part of the country that's known as God's own

6

So they cultivate grain on an altar in Chile
and use an old cannon to keep milk on ice
and then they make kindling of poison-tipped arrows
and use a lost bastion for growing their rice

And then they play ball games with innocent bombshells
And hide-and-go-seek in a closed parliament
And then they play chess with the minuscule pieces
Of what at one time was a great president

So they cultivate grapes in the stony old Mafia
And slaughter their sheep and goats inside the banks
And then they drive Rolls-Royces all around Sofia
And they burn rubles and dollars and francs

And then they sing songs of the joy of the people
And songs of the grief of the people as well
And then they blow off all the parties and topple
The last paper tiger from his citadel

7

Many the people who've dreamed a society
sat there and dreamed in a driving rain
dreamed of a sun rising from an abyss
to warm every person and show him a sign

Suddenly he is the happy machine
Suddenly his own imaginings are wild
Suddenly he is the one who is laughing
Suddenly he is entirely stilled

Suddenly he makes a run for his life
Suddenly he has a word that strikes home
Suddenly he takes the whole thing for granted
Suddenly he knows just what he wants done

The truth is a process we try to keep hidden
but no one can hide a splintered process
And faith will live on in the darkest of caverns
And faith will live on in the purest excess

8

Life is holy

1

There are basilisks with wings of stone
crowned stones that move

crowns of gold for the holy
fables of the freedom of matter

holy stone-litanies grinding
deep under layers of culture

new life in the forsaken desert
a basis of bloom hallelujah

asymmetry of visions

2

There are darknesses with solar flares
paralyzed fools

psychoses suddenly resolved
over 100 miles a second

miracles of kindness
shattering the social framework

the fool steps out of his image
lights a candle in bright sunlight

desire to see the invisible

3

There are forests of violent fevertrees
known for their speedy growth

one morning suddenly foliage
unfolding enchanted lovely

a global temperature increase
luxuriance in all sexes

people communicate as if possessed
hurricanes of images rushing

parliaments flow with honey

4

There are Marxists with feet of clay
prematurely born as colossi

if they make a sudden leap
the sea washes them away

for the fluctuating stock index reigns
the battle for the seller's market

the war to ensure peace
between the parties of the labor market

age of the great religious wars

5

There are lesbian feminists
hefty flesh-worshiping matrons

Bernini figures set free
baying swans

land in a plaza during siesta
line up for a protest march

naked procession through the streets
Clytemnestra in the lead

pure provocation

6

There are prophecies of paradise
the lion at rest with the lamb

euphoric favorable milieus
sheltered childhoods

scents of illness
old hospital bouquets

stale water
catatonia

better a swift earthly kick

7

There are feverish manifestos
offerings of flowers and wine

white-clad doves in cages
virgins hidden in coffins

migratory anecdotes carried on
from high to high

grass that turns brains green
blithering beauty

the original political initiative

8

There are panegyric celebrations
the graves are opened too soon

the people abandon the factory
the stench of the corpses clings

a man leaps onto a pillar
jubilation and praise

soldiers and police open fire
what shall we do

life is holy

> Eternity is in love with the
> productions of time
> William Blake

1

1. They go out into a desert and meet energy

2. Time measurable on the whole only in terms of life

3. For instance the word desolation is in itself a denial of itself

4. Heat.   The osmotic pressure between body and air vanishes

5. A human made of sand.   A human setting a desert of sand in motion

6. Every substance on earth in the body.   A high producing our love

> If the fool would persist in his
> folly he would become wise
>   William Blake

2

1. Crying to high heaven.   That's them.

2. As freely as only a conflict formulates its stable model

3. A pulse with no body

4. He lies down on the welcome mat outside the lovers' door

5. She refuses to eat until they understand

6. Better insanity than loathing for others

>   If the Sun & Moon should doubt
>   They'd immediately Go out
>   William Blake

3

1. They sleep together like a tree leafing out

2. The pollen-dusted summer that rises from the dust

3. The complete silence of language about everything that doesn't happen

4. Excess motion as a sign of life

5. Excess formulation as a sign of life

6. They are burning. They are immortal

> In her trembling hands she took
> The new born terror howling
> William Blake

4

1. I do call out to you when I think you're leaving me

2. In the hidden passages between life and death

3. I will not pretend that I am dead. I am afraid

4. I accept my powerlessness because I deny it

5. Singing. Off into the blue

6. We survive only because we use words

> Exuberance is beauty
> William Blake

5

1. They dance in the streets. They have flowers in their mouths

2. To cover random death with random life

3. As during high fevers the delight of meaning nothing

4. They talk with strangers

5. Not comparing but creating their own metamorphosis

6. They know there is enough. More than enough.

> God made Man happy and Rich, but
> The Subtil made the innocent
> Poor
>
> William Blake

6

1. All we own is stolen from each other

2. As if a human were not a human

3. The world inside me as the matter we share with each other

4. We share a meal

5. We literally share existence

6. To live as though there were hope and a future

> I then asked Ezekiel why he eat
> dung & lay so long on his right
> & left side? he answer'd, "the
> desire of raising other men in-
> to a perception of the infinite"
> William Blake

7

1. They go to war for each other   Against each other

2. Meanwhile while they still have excess enough to dole out death so
   slowly that it looks like life they try to love each other's hatred

3. It's you It's me It's the disagreements between us

4. Naked as John and Yoko Ono

5. Jesus who tells a fantastic story: Cheers!

6. We are all semaphores for each other

> . . . all that has existed in the space of six thousand years,
> permanent & not lost nor vanished, & every little act,
> word, work & wish that has existed, all remaining still
>   William Blake

8

1. We work with the others on something or other

2. Someone breaks into a house and lives there as long as possible

3. Happiness is the change that comes over me when I describe the world
    It comes over the world

4. We are caught up in each other's lives

5. We live on in each other

6. The validity of relationships is condensed and shifted

1

And around goes the happy machine
    With a man who is white and eats salt

Where is he going? He's going nowhere
    His words and his excrement are stars

2

And around goes the wild imagination
    With a man who plucks out angels' feathers

What shall he do?   What else?
    He has such nice talks with the sky

3

And around goes the fantastic din
    With a man who sets fire to himself

What shall he say?   Is there more to say?
    It's a matter of grace

4

And around goes the wheel standing still
    With a man who is running amok

Where is he going?   Probably nowhere
    His body a gift to the earth

5

And around it goes and no one feels it
    The man has ejaculated

He talks with everyone   He embraces everyone
    The women give birth

6

And around it goes as you run for your life
    Life must not vanish

Why should it vanish?
    When everyone has caught up with everyone

7

And around goes the word that strikes home
     And all are struck by its silence

8

And around it goes and the dogs bark

1

last seen on the screen/stop/in Prague/stop/read aloud from a Russian news-
paper/stop/subtitled/stop/subtitles muddled/stop/jubilation/stop/his major
works/stop/about traumatic chemistry of system/stop/15 copies/stop/natural
political consciousness/stop/in everyone/stop/offprints/stop/obscene scrib-
blings/stop/on an old telephone pad/stop/salvaged/stop/should be
published/stop/deported/stop/publicity/stop/ritual should be followed/stop/
follow utopian ideal/stop/do not know him/stop/he must have a function/stop/

2

rm. 319/stop/orders from room service/stop/has shutters closed/stop/is
armed/stop/intercepted/stop/telegrams/stop/are lyrical/stop/about his metabo-
lism/stop/he loves a geisha/stop/Japan/stop/*you know*/stop/brags about his
erection/stop/in Brooklyn/stop/Evelyn/stop/married/stop/to a lawyer/stop/
Miller/stop/27 Commercial Road/stop/feels like his head is bursting/stop/too
much gas in bowels/stop/it's all the geisha's fault/stop/a code/stop/ lung
cancer/stop/but does it mean anything to us/stop/other than aesthetically/stop/

3

he lunches with the Buddha/stop/must be some new strategy/stop/for one thing
they have planted a tree/stop/has not come up/stop/insist they are in the shade/
stop/sunstroke/stop/burns/stop/their lunch invisible/stop/air-knives air-forks/
stop/eating description/stop/emptiness/stop/nirvana/stop/forestall rumors/
stop/eat this telegram/stop/

4

map of area/stop/trees listed/stop/but not tree he is under/stop/he talks like an owl/stop/he laughs/stop/hash/stop/have talked with him/stop/was there when tree came up/stop/an image/stop/difficult to substantiate/stop/he says police are fiction/stop/*you know*/stop/

5

have followed them/stop/in car/stop/to woods/stop/on foot out to tree/stop/
listing will follow/stop/duel/stop/reporting/stop/tall one/stop/"leap says the
world"/stop/dark one/stop/"the world stands completely still"/stop/bullets
straight through brain/stop/both still lying there/stop/check Marx/stop/
awaiting orders/stop/

6

nothing new/stop/have tailed him/stop/usually sits in cafes/stop/whistling/
stop/same tune each time/stop/melody will follow/stop/11 a.m./stop/gave up
studying morphology/stop/3 p.m./stop/bought a magnet/stop/plays with it/
stop/big baby/stop/just slipped out/stop/he didn't hear/stop/5 p.m./stop/
retort/stop/hey world/stop/7 p.m./stop/he repeated/stop/hey world/stop/was
whistling/stop/must figure out system/stop/

7

has met her/stop/they talk/stop/and make love/stop/at same time/stop/
completely fantastic activity/stop/no more to say about it/stop-

8

hey clown/stop/it's all within reach/stop/the stage/stop/ready/stop/has never been so big/stop/hey/stop/

1

Inside the first factory there is a second, inside the second there is a third, inside the third a fourth factory etc.

Inside factory no. 3517 a man stands by a machine

In factory no. 1423 a man stands by a machine

Man no. 8611 has been spinning fables all this time about freedom

At the end of all the united factories stands a man making money

2

Inside the first barrack there is a second, inside the second there is a third, inside the third a fourth barrack etc.

Inside barrack no. 3517 the men are stacked in heaps

In barrack no. 1423 the men are completely identical

Man no. 8611 has been spinning fables all this time about peace

At the end of all the united barracks sits a mad general

3

Inside the first institution there is a second, inside the second there is a third, inside the third a fourth institution etc.

In institution no. 3517 they keep everyone who is definitely abnormal

In institution no. 1423 individuals who say the abnormal are normal

Man no. 8611 has been spinning fables all this time about a society

At the end of all the united institutions sits a committee of experts

4

Inside the first parliament there is a second, inside the second there is a third, inside the third a fourth parliament etc.

In parliament no. 3517 power is being discussed

In parliament no. 1423 power is being discussed

Man no. 8611 has been spinning fables all this time about a little more imagination

At the end of all the united parliaments sits a well-paid advisor

5

Inside the first office there is a second, inside the second there is a third, inside the third a fourth office etc.

Inside office no. 3517 an advisor advises an administrator

In office no. 1423 an administrator administers an advisor

Man no. 8611 has been spinning fables all this time about consideration

At the end of all the united offices sits a well-paid hidden observer

6

Inside the first bank there is a second, inside the second there is a third, inside the third a fourth bank etc.

Inside bank no. 3517 a man calculates war expenditures

In bank no. 1425 a man calculates war profits

Man no. 8611 has been spinning fables all this time about fair distribution

At the end of all the united banks sits a smart speculator

7

Inside the first company there is a second, inside the second company there is a third, inside the third a fourth company etc.

Inside company no. 3517 a man calculates a worker's output

In company no. 1423 a man calculates a worker's life expectancy

Man no. 8611 has been spinning fables all this time about the individual's right to his own life

At the end of all the united companies sits a financial dynasty

8

Inside the first society there is a second, inside the second there is a third, inside the third a fourth society etc.

Inside society no. 3517 a man contemplates a society

In society no. 1423 a man contemplates a society

Man no. 8611 has been spinning fables all this time about happiness

At the end of all the united societies sits Mr. _____ smiling, *"I'm very pleased to meet you. You are my very first patient"*

1

They line up clock in and change clothes
They talk about the weather It hasn't been too cold
It's cold in the factory But it did rain a little
At exactly 6 a.m. they have to be in their places
There are no windows—that matters too
Of course cold is something you can get used to
But it's a long time until 3 p.m. Wonder if it'll rain
They change clothes and line up and clock out

2

They have private lockers for their personal things
Money and keys for instance And any letters a person might get
At first some turned their backs
When they took off their pants And some laughed
And at first of course the beds were too close
And at first they talked so loudly
How would it feel to shoot a human being
Now they all read their letters to each other

3

They tie them to the beds when they get restless
No one understands them
The people who tie them seem restless too
They do what they can
When they are relatively calm they sit in the halls
One of them might tell a story
For instance he might claim that the water they're drinking
Is wine Then they all laugh and get roaring drunk

4

Those attending have to endure a long string of speeches
Meanwhile some talk Or some read or sleep
One of them might make notes or mutter to himself
He has to give a speech on Thursday
If only a few more would show up
Most are outside the main hall at meetings
The voices sound like it's important
Impossible to hear what they're saying

5

Most call each other by first names It's more practical
Besides it creates a relaxed atmosphere
And they are going to be together for most of their lives
Of course some would rather not have to
But that's all right There's not supposed to be pressure
When someone has a birthday they buy a round
In February an important paper disappeared
They think it's exciting Who could have done it

6

When customers come in they must speak more quietly to each other
Then their footsteps sound louder
That makes some people uneasy
That's why the floors are made of marble
Fresh bouquets are put on the counters every Tuesday
But that's something new
And of course someone had to be funny
Good to see there's something around besides honesty

7

They come right in and look it all over
They talk about the weather It hasn't been too cold
There's money in most things But it did rain a little
At exactly 10 a.m. they have to be in their places
The fact that they're there matters only to them
Of course money is something you have to get used to
But it's a long time until 3 p.m. Wonder if it'll rain
When they've looked it all over they go home

8

Occasionally they meet on the street
Or run into each other in a bar
Most of them do know each other
Or know of each other
Then they usually talk about the ruling classes
A lot of people think that the oppressed
Love to follow the standards of the rulers
It's fairly standard to talk about that kind of thing

1

On the first day they invented sand. And the sand settled into itself, just as they thought it would. After the sand had settled, they tried it out to see if it could be walked on. It could. When they walked they sank in a little, but not enough to worry about. And they saw that they left marks in the sand. Every step they took left marks in the sand. They called them footprints. Now it was easier to see where they had walked. That was good. And they hadn't invented wind and rain, so the footprints stayed where they were. That way others could follow them. If any others should want to. And that would be good. So on the very first day they made a lot of footprints in the sand. The whole first day they walked around and made footprints in the sand. When they really had made a lot of footprints in the sand, they sat down to rest and to enjoy the results of their efforts. They looked over the endless expanse and described it to each other. And when they were through describing it to each other and had no more to say to each other, either about the sand or about the many footprints they had made in the endless expanse, they saw that something was missing. And one of them said: I go in and out of this desert whenever I want

2

On the second day they invented light. And the light spread by itself, as they had thought it would. When the light was through spreading and there was light everywhere, they saw that they could see the sand. And they immediately began to describe what they saw. Yellow and brown, they said. And green and blue and red, they said. And black and white, they said. And gray, they said. And they said it a lot of times. Finally they really felt that they were all seeing the same thing. And that was good. A little later they saw that they could also see each other. We can see each other, they said. Just like that. And because they had said it just like that, they felt that they were all seeing the same thing. And that was good. In the middle of the day, when the light was very strong, they realized the light was very strong, and they closed their eyes and sat down in the sand to rest and to keep from getting lost. They had never imagined that the light would be so strong. It's taken over, they said. And while they sat there in the sand with their eyes closed, they really did suffer in the heat of all the light they had invented. They hadn't invented wind and rain, remember. So there was no coolness at all. Let's look away from it all for a moment, one of them said. So they did. And they really felt that they were all seeing the same thing. I can visualize the light, they said. That was how they suddenly understood that they had loved each other all along.

3

On the third day they invented water. If they hadn't, the water might have appeared by itself. It looks like it appeared by itself, they said. And they tried it out, to see if it could be walked on. It couldn't. They kept falling through. And when they went back to the sand their feet were wet, and the sand stuck to them. So they sat down and brushed the sand from their feet. At first it was hard because the sand was wet. Little by little it got easier because the sand dried. So they talked together about the sand and the water and their effects on each other. And they realized that they had felt the sand back on the first day. It had vanished between their fingers. So they felt the water. It vanished between their fingers. Finally they felt the light. It was as if our fingers were vanishing, they said. And they felt that now they had proof of their love.

4

On the fourth day they invented grass. When the grass was as green as they thought it would be, they saw that they couldn't see the sand. And all the footprints they had made in the endless expanse had vanished. There were birds in the air, there were fish in the water, and when they lay down in the grass they could feel its movement on their skin. It was nice. But even though it was nice, they were all alone in the world. And even if any others should want to, they would never be able to find them. Since the footprints had vanished and the endless expanse was covered with grass. So they sat up and discussed the situation that had come up. At last they agreed to set off through the grass and see what happened. Nothing happened. The whole fourth day they walked through the grass, and where the grass was tall they held hands so they wouldn't lose each other, but nothing happened. They left no footprints, and the grass closed in behind them, and they were walking away from the water. And they understood that more was missing than they had originally thought.

5

On the fifth day they invented summer heat. When the summer heat had reached its height as they had thought it would, they were at peace with themselves. They didn't know why they had invented the summer heat. It was completely super-fluous. During the middle of the day the light was already so strong that it was stronger than the strongest summer heat. But maybe they had forgotten that they had invented light. In the same way they had begun to get thirsty after they had invented water. And especially after they had walked away from the water. Why do we always do things that are superfluous and useless, they said. But as soon as they had spoken they understood that there were far too many questions. It's this superfluity that constitutes the truth, they said. And if any others should want to, they would be able to find us. And they would love us, because loving us is super-fluous. That's how they will invent us, sooner or later. And they saw that nothing was missing at all.

6

On the sixth day they invented paper. When the paper was as white as they had thought it would be, they saw that they couldn't see the sand or the light or the water. At last they couldn't see the grass either. And the summer heat had long since vanished. It was a very dangerous situation. It was the most dangerous situation they had been in yet. There was paper absolutely everywhere. All that paper is superfluous, they said. And they looked over the endless expanse. It was white. They had actually never thought it would be so white. It's taken over, they said. And besides there's nothing but paper, they said. That's how they described everything. Yellow and brown, they wrote. And green and blue and red, they wrote. And black and white, they wrote. And gray, they wrote. And they wrote it a lot of times. At last they really felt that they were all writing the same thing. And when they were completely sure that they were all writing the same thing, they began to write about the first and second day, about the sand and the light. And they wrote about the third and fourth day, about the water and the grass. And they wrote about the fifth day, about the summer heat. Finally they wrote about the paper. And they really felt that they were all writing the same thing. And that was good.

7

On the seventh day they invented snow. And the snow settled into itself, just as they thought it would. After the snow had settled, they tried it out to see if it could be walked on. It could. When they walked they sank in a little, but not enough to worry about. And they saw that they had left marks in the snow. Every step they took left marks in the snow. They called them footprints. Now it was easier to see where they had walked. That was good. And they hadn't invented wind and rain, so the footprints stayed where they were. That way others could follow them. If any others should want to. And that would be good. So on the very seventh day they made a lot of footprints in the snow. When they really had made a lot of footprints in the snow, they sat down to rest and to enjoy the results of their efforts. They looked over the endless expanse and described it to each other. And when they were through describing it to each other and had no more to say to each other, either about the snow or about the many footprints they had made in the endless expanse, they saw that everything was covered with snow. It will all come out by itself, they said, when the snow melts.

8

On the eighth day they invented beds. They rested the whole eighth day and made love with each other. It was nice. That's how they finally became super-fluous enough.

1

There at the center of the boundless garden
The boundaries are still in place, unchanging
And blood count, pressure, pulse have sharply fallen

The bodies make a few attempts at crying
Without tear-pressure, though, it doesn't matter
Just sex organs have moisture still remaining

White stretchers bear the bodies that they gather
All raving that the right to joy is sure
For only utter fools would spout such blather

(The skeleton the feelings all secure)

2

The doctor drives the last part of their tour
They masturbate their skeletons As noted
He helps them to that pleasure, clear and pure

When they arrive the air is saturated
With tears and semen, mucus, clouds, and water
The atmosphere so highly concentrated

The orgasm makes normal cities quiver

3

The doctor has dropped acid and endeavors
To greet the patients, show the way ahead
And clarify appropriate procedures

When all is said and done, we all are dead
Midway upon the journey of our life
Our life is stupid ugly desolate

So do not fear The facts confirm that if
We lose perspective we can find relief

4

Well that's the way he spoke   He raised the knife
Sliced pieces out of all the greatest visions
And laughed and shouted, kittenish and blithe

Hey hey now I'm a lightning bolt that's spreading
A strong electric jolt from all your bedding

5

In due time the first sorrow filtered out
There in the hospital hallway, a simple
Snort as from a pig with lowered snout

And everyone perceived it as a signal
For fear and freedom, love and pain to start
So each employee turned into a rebel

6

They ran outside and shouted   See my heart
It beats a sentence underneath my skin
I want so very much to love your pain

7

The patients pressed against the window glass
To watch their new friends take this drastic measure
They knew it was impossible unless

The sick possessed put the world under pressure

8

The small sick dirty murders of the world

1

They can't go saying they don't see me. Because I love them and I just want them all to be happy. So I know they can see me perfectly well. Yesterday was an especially bad day. When they came and got me. They said that if I cried my blood pressure was too low. And if I didn't cry my pulse was too slow. I don't think they understood me. We drove through the garden. And I tried to explain to them that I didn't need to be tied to the stretcher. Don't you love the flowers, I said. Yes, of course we do, they said. But I don't think they understood me. One of them said, this is really a paradise for these people. It's almost too good. We have a lot of them who even get permission to have normal sex lives. They apparently thought I couldn't remember such long sentences. Otherwise they probably wouldn't have said that. But now at any rate they can't go saying they don't see me. After all, I'm in Paradise. I can tell I really am in Paradise just by the simple fact that there are tons of sand everywhere. And on the first day they did invent sand. It's in big containers all over the place. They're for peeing in. Last night I sneaked out and fastened a little note to one of them: (The skeleton the feelings all secure) But I don't think they understood me. At any rate they tied me down again. But I am allowed to write. I don't care for Paradise. I go in and out of this paradise whenever I want.

2

Today I asked for some more paper. My excuse was that I had forgotten to tell my wife something yesterday. Or if I am a woman, I had forgotten to tell my husband something. I just want to tell you that Paradise is a boundless garden, but you don't have to worry about coming in and getting lost or anything like that because the boundaries are still in place, unchanging, and it's easy to tell when you get to them because they really did invent light and there's light everywhere. Someone is looking over my shoulder as I write this. And now he's asking if it's a code. Which is why I answer him by asking, Why are you always masturbating right on your skeleton? But I don't think he understood me. It was referred to as an episode and the light was off for a long time. Of course it just meant that I loved him. Sometimes that kind of thing has to be said in code. Otherwise people get frightened. When the light came back I saw that he was still standing there. We can see each other, I said. I said that because I didn't want him to think that what I'd said before was intended to be mean. But he never cries. So I don't think he understood me.

3

Now I've been trying to concentrate on my project of explaining why we're happy and why we love each other. It can't be done without pain. But we can take each other's pain into consideration, and even if we can't do anything at the moment, we can always make up for that later on when we have time. There is no one we cannot do something for, even though it is impossible. Later the doctor said he was crazy himself. But I understood right away that it was just to get me to identify with him. I can't. One reason is that I'm not crazy. I just want people to understand that they love each other. And another is that he doesn't mean it seriously. So I won't play his game either. That's why I said to him, You're not crazy at all. You're dead. But he just kept on the way he'd started and said, When all is said and done we all are dead. I could see what he was up to. He wanted us to go through the whole process together and lose perspective. But it's also a political issue. And even though he tried to get into his role, talking about water and semen and clouds and mucus and saying that he was the one who had invented water, I knew perfectly well that he could never be crazy. Because he thinks it's possible to do things for people. But I didn't say that. I said, There is no one we cannot do something for, even though it is impossible.

4

Today certain difficulties have come up. As you know they invented grass. Today someone peed in the grass, and then the grass just gets too high, because the grass is supposed to reach only a certain height. That's why we're supposed to pee in the sand, in the containers set up for that. But it's also a political issue. Because the grass mustn't get so high that it closes in behind people and you can't tell the difference between them. I want so much to get out of here; there are always so many things happening to distract me. For instance today while we were making our beds one of the doctors came running in with a knife in his hand. Hey hey I'm a lightning bolt, he shouted, slicing all our bedding to shreds. Then he sat down in a corner and laughed and shouted and acted completely kittenish and blithe, almost like a young girl. But I don't think any of us believed him. It was probably something they staged so that the business about keeping us off the grass wouldn't make us get too aggressive.

5

I'm going to have to ask you to bring in my papers with the license for us to love each other. Don't feel bad; you know I love you no matter what. But they have to use them in a test. One of the others went through a test today. You're a pig, they told him; please lower your snout and snort. Of course they're right; it is amazing that we always do things that are superfluous and useless, but I just don't think that was what they had in mind. It was out in the hallway with a lot of the employees around and the man really did it. But afterward we could all see the sorrow in his eyes. I can't answer for what would happen if the employees and patients got together one day and formulated the urge to rebel that filled us. Love is strong. And that snort was really a signal. I know this may prolong my stay, but I couldn't resist threatening the doctor on duty. But he just smiled and acted like he was off in his own world and said, Midway upon the journey of our life, our life is stupid ugly desolate. He still doesn't want to believe that I see through him. I know perfectly well that he's not crazy; he's just literary. I told him that, too. But he just shook his head and wrote it down, adding in parentheses: condition worsened due to summer heat.

6

Today I've asked permission to be left alone. I was afraid I'd go crazy and forget about my project. I also asked for some more paper, but at first they acted like they didn't understand me; but then I acted like I was crazy and ran around shouting, See my heart It beats a sentence underneath my skin And when a cleaning lady said that what I was saying sounded very beautiful, they got scared and gave me a lot of paper. Of course they'll never admit that they got scared. They'll just be glad to have more material to file away and use against me. I could strangle them and escape. I would make up for it later. There is no one we cannot do something for, even though it is impossible. At any rate, now I have a lot of paper. I am truly grateful that they invented paper. I know that agitation is prohibited. That's why I'm writing so beautifully. But I'm sure they understand it. I want so very much to love your pain, I write. I've written it on reams of paper and secretly handed them out to the patients and the employees, both. Now we'll see what happens.

7

Today all the patients agreed to say it was snowing. We all took our places by the windows and pressed our faces to the glass and exclaimed joyously over the snow and described it and dreamed about how wonderful it would be to play in it. Meanwhile the sun was shining away and the doctors got confused by our total agreement and couldn't figure out if they should act like they were crazy and say it was snowing or act like they were crazy and say it wasn't snowing. Meanwhile we saw the employees leap into the garden and run around acting like it was full of snow. I don't know if our agitating had helped or if they were just taking advantage of the general confusion to get a break and go outside and fool around and enjoy the sun. But it really doesn't matter. Because the press showed up and took pictures of the employees running around and throwing snowballs and sledding and making snowmen and rolling each other in the snow. In the newspapers it said that all the employees had gone crazy. They had flowers in their hair and dirt and grass all over them. It's that kind of thing that puts pressure on the world. And one of them laughed right into the TV camera and shouted, I want so very much to love your pain. Even though things may be back to normal tomorrow, I don't think any of them will forget that.

8

Today I've been in bed all day. You know they invented beds. And today they tied us all down. It's clear that they want to punish us for yesterday. Now I know you'll immediately mutter something about all the small sick dirty murders of the world and start planning a quick takeover. But I want to ask you to relax. We're all right, and they can't hold out much longer with us lying here like this. Because we're just resting and making love with each other. And even though we can't touch each other, it's nice.

Wir brauchen nicht erst lange
nachzuforschen, eine leichte
Vergleichung, nur wenige Züge im
Sande sind genug, um uns zu ver-
ständingen. So ist uns alles eine
grosse Schrift . . . . .
                                        Novalis

1

A great many of the bodily functions will be especially suitable for demonstration. This holds true primarily for the functions of the glands and the digestive organs, but also for the movements of the sex organs when they are not impinged upon. The exposed surfaces can be observed with the naked eye, moving as a simple consequence of the workings of the underlying heart. But we can go further, and while still lying outstretched in the sand we can mentally review the skeletal system: skull, vertebral column, pelvic girdle, together with the appended limbs. But without losing touch with the feelings. In addition it is noteworthy that one can feel secure throughout the procedure simply because one might just as easily have lain anywhere else. Later we can move closer to each other and begin the actual touching.

Die Sprache ist Delphi.
                    Novalis

2

During the actual touching it is important to formulate one's impressions freely. One must simply remember that tears, sighs, cries, laughter, and humming are part of formulation, and that the code used can depend heavily at times on the linguistic physiologies of the bodies involved. During the climax of the inter-course itself a brief moment can occur that is not describable with either positive or negative turns of phrase. I have heard people who became frightened say it was as if their toes had taken over the faculty of formulation and they themselves were gone. That is expressed somewhat awkwardly, but it shows that there is nothing to be afraid of. After all, this is what one lay waiting for countless times while still alone.

Jede Krankheit ist ein musika-
lisches Problem
Novalis

3

Nevertheless the majority will still be afraid. That can only be called natural, even more so when one takes into account that fear is an experience, not a neurosis. For that reason, when they go out into the squares and streets and carry out their projects, the demonstrators must be advised not to hide anything. At first of course their nakedness will attract attention, but in reality it is their fear and joy that people will have come to see. And it is very important that people have an opportunity to experience something they know. Aside from that, it is also a political issue. People must learn to experience politics as something natural: There is no one we cannot do something for, even though it is impossible.

*Sich nach den Dingen oder die
Dinge nach sich richten—ist
Eins*

Novalis

4

Of course certain difficulties may arise. In many places walking on the grass will
be prohibited, and in a few places the grass will be so high that no one can see
what is happening. In most places there will be no grass at all; the surface can
thus be termed hard and unsuitable, asphalt for instance or paving stones, side-
walks, and stairs. The demonstrators are therefore advised to bring along their
own mats. Should they encounter further difficulties—for instance, should rolling
out their mats be prohibited—the majority will undoubtedly be able to carry out
their projects without mats, perhaps standing up. Furthermore, should the
process itself be prohibited, there will undoubtedly be ways to comply. Ultimately
of course it will succeed. There is no cause for panic, no cause for aggression in
response to any prohibitions.

Menschheit ist eine humoristi-
sche Rolle

Novalis

5

If individual demonstrators are arrested it may—I emphasize may—be to their advantage to ask immediately to be allowed to put on some clothing, perhaps their own. And if the arrested individual encounters remarks such as You are a pig, it will undoubtedly be to his advantage to do no more than nod agreement. In due time when the matter is reported in the newspapers it will evoke a strong sympathy in someone for human beings, in any case. If, on the other hand, he encounters a remark such as And you are a human being, no one can answer right away for what will happen, especially if the newspaper readers and the demonstrator get together and formulate the urge to rebel that fills them. To all appearances they cherish a strong sympathy for life as such.

Bosheit ist nichts als eine Ge-
mütskrankheit die in der Ver-
nunft ihren Sitz hat und daher
so hartnäckig und nur durch ein
Wunder zu heilen ist.

Novalis

6

In this context it is interesting to note that every activity carried out within the bounds of reason is in reality unreasonable, because it either comes to a dead end or is worked out automatically, with no disorder. Whereas the completely unreasonable activity is in reality reasonable, because it ends in a vision and automatically creates disorder in all our memories (*in all our minds*). So when a demonstrator in his cell learns that he is there to have his reason restored, that demonstrator must be advised to ask for a large quantity of paper. When he begins to write on it, he must choose his words with care, so that his writings are markedly strange and beautiful. If this succeeds and the writings are censored, he will immediately be released. For the guards on all shifts have orders that whenever possible they are to perceive as reasonable everything strange and beautiful, as long as it is written on a large quantity of paper. They are not evil. They just cannot see that there is anything to wonder at.

*Gemeinschaftlicher Wahnsinn hört
auf, Wahnsinn zu sein und wird
Magie, Wahnsinn nach Regeln und
mit vollem Bewusstsein.*

Novalis

7

In the beginning a marked tendency simply to act insane will be noticed in the individual demonstrator. The mere fact that he is naked will cause him to want to hide in the norm of insanity. But as soon as he touches the other demonstrators and they roll each other in the snow or in feelings and get up and pair off and dance and formulate their impressions freely—flowers in their hair and dirt and grass all over them—he will understand that it is a kind of insanity to act as if the individual exists. It is this understanding that must of necessity be disciplined. In order to keep the movement soft at all times, the individual must be hard on himself. Insanity is the ability to do the impossible. Magic is the will to.

Ich bin Du
Novalis

8

As mentioned previously, one's location does not matter. One must simply try consciously to aim straight into the impossible. Of course one must stay balanced as one goes. But only on the condition that balance is made uncertain. Increasingly uncertain.

1

After the first morning I seek
the lips' crude formulations

Again and again I kiss the memory of
pass me!   pass me!   The salt and the white
consciousness in endless writing

What you gave my thoughts is words and
excrement, a body with the functions
of a star

What you gave me is pure morning

My passion: to go further

2

After the second morning I seek
the lips' raving joy

Again and again I formulate the wind
so it has nice talks with the sky and
an angel is wild among us

What you gave my thoughts is the blindness
of sex, a need for
awkward expression

What you gave me is pure imagination

My passion: to go further

3

After the third morning I seek
the lips' sweet music

Again and again I arouse joy so that
there is a fantastic din and
fire sets fire to itself

What you gave my thoughts is the movements
of fear, the restfulness of doing
the impossible

What you gave me is pure grace

My passion: to go further

4

After the fourth morning I seek
the lips' speechless expression

Again and again I stand completely
still so the wheel goes around and
there's no cause for panic

What you gave my thoughts is no-
where, with a body that's a
gift to the earth

What you gave me is pure rest/restlessness

My passion: to go further

5

After the fifth morning I seek
the lips' lighthearted message

Again and again I nod agreement
take me! take me! so no one can answer
for what happens next

What you gave my thoughts is a strong
sympathy for life as such
hey

What you gave me is pure vanishing

My passion: to go further

6

After the sixth morning I seek
the lips' true confusion

Again and again I run for my life because
life must not vanish and every-
one must catch up to everyone

What you gave my thoughts is the closeness
of absence, a wonder that I live
my life

What you gave me is nonstop wonder

My passion: to go further

7

After the seventh morning I seek
the rules of the lips' insanity

Again and again I roll in the snow and
get up freely and formulate my
words that strike home

What you gave my thoughts is the insanity
of feelings, the strength in the soft
movements

What you gave me is shared magic

My passion: to go further

8

After the eighth morning I seek
and find

Again and again I aim straight
into the impossible The dogs bark
and around it all goes

What you gave my thoughts is pure
confusion, balance that's uncertain/
certain

What you gave me is all the impossible

My passion: to go further

1

In the silence of the writing/the silence of the writer
the terrifying silence-machine of what is written

The world vanishes/world after world
vanishes/slips into a world

of polished silences/into a world
of marble skeletons/into the frozen

canopies amoebas and sex organs/into
the blown-out skulls lost touches

into the heart/into the brain
into the painted bowels and cardboard

glands/into the thoughts' plaster housing
the hard concrete blocks of the muscles

the steel of the feelings/like a construction site
sounds from a thundering silence

2

How to integrate the razed building
How to guide writing into place in its chaos

The dust is thick/and beneath it the rubble
of toppled statues/bodies in preporno-

graphic positions/the clamor of the languishing
gazes/the helplessly outstretched hands

How to integrate a world
completely and hopelessly ended

into a world that will not begin
How to integrate thunder

into silence/The lovers look at
the disinfected sorrow-surfaces/all the minute

forgotten mind-starts/and they are deeply touched
at the sight of a foot broken off with toes intact

3

Who are the lovers/any and all
generously spreading their virus around

persisting in their fear/even
when those in power kiss them

even when those in power pair off with them
and cram their love into the bargain

all who play music/all who play
their fever through/so it catches

fire throughout the world/so it heals all
who catch it/any and all/all who

are enthroned on the pillar of despair *why not*
all who experience something they know

from their own experience/all who persist in
it all/even though it is impossible

4

Things comply with the lovers/be-
cause the lovers comply with things

if making love is prohibited/the lovers
comply with the prohibition and call it

something else/when those in power arrive
at the scene of the crime/they see only

the dust and the toppled statues/the helpless
hands and the skulls' broken edges/the whole

illiterate passion/and smile
everything is stifled/the very process

as such is shattered/everything is ridiculous
old ruins and muteness/they do not see

all the naked demonstrators/who tenderly
press themselves against the broken marble figures

5

When those in power arrest a pillar
despair moves out onto a ledge

when those in power arrest a bowel
an organ a gland/the lovers pass

gas and make love and sweat with all the re-
maining parts of themselves/when those in

power arrest a foot that continues
to express the experience of the body/the

lovers inch along on their stomachs/walk on their
hands/stand on their heads/secrete words

that run around by themselves/words
with a strong sympathy for life as such

When those in power arrest a humanity
power moves out onto a ledge

6

Those in power are not evil/but it will take
a wonder to make them see anything beautiful

in the foot they have standing on their table
how can it be made into a vision/how

can an eloquent broken-off foot
bring disorder to their minds

their view of things is so hardheaded
that they can see only what is unreasonable in

the foot/not the foot in what is unreasonable
so it will take a wonder/it will take

a wonder/perhaps a refined torture
of reason/for instance if the newspapers

used the word love in place of power
that would make you wonder

7

When the insane roll in the dust
when they hug a plastic amoeba close

to them and sing the praises of the culture
when they pick up the toppled statues

and bear them together in procession
single broken fragments or whole skeletons

when they lift the frozen canopies
from the Pentagon the Kremlin the world

and raise them high over the finest statue
of the president speaker general

and write the one word love
in the middle of his gleaming forehead

then love is probably compromised
but power is transformed

8

This is how the lovers are off balance
to keep the world in balance

This is how the lovers are afraid
because the president is happy

This is how the lovers are above everything
because the president has said there are limits

This is how the lovers go into the impossible
because the president goes for what is possible

This is how the lovers go for the president
I am you I am you

Here and now
Here and now

1

as sand vanishing
to nothing in wind
have any save none
lived for so long

I ran to meet you
dying on

2

as light that can never
see itself
as none can lie still
falling free

I see your eyes
see

3

as water that bears
itself to death
you give what is yours
time that goes

semen
tears

4

as the grass growing
into your body
the body withering
into its mind

mind spreading out
over skin

5

as warmth as a summer
remembered to emptiness
we dream of joy
unknown unguessed

and into us looked
something else than ourselves

6

as paper at rest
while a word passes
sorrow gone white
joy in its blackness

I want to know nothing
you walk by my side

7

as snow in its purity
white and alone
only a few days
only a few

and ever
the earth returns

8

as the bed opening
and closing open
darkness and light
I am cold I am hot

the body preserves
its world

1

I see that I'm sitting and writing
See what is being written What was written
Read and see what has been read
See the silence again ahead
See it tune in to my writing
Vanish into what was written/what is writing
Read itself
Begin to shout to itself

2

I see that I have a lot of trouble
With what happens by itself anyway
I see that I have a lot of trouble
Because it happens by itself anyway
I see that I'm rushing toward the point
Where everything happens by itself anyway
If I'm not rushing toward the point
I can't even see that it happens by itself

3

I see that I understand too much
I see that I'm getting into death
As if I understood it well
As if it would be fine
For death to understand me well
For death to be getting into me
I see that I'm running a fever
I see that I'm afraid

4

I see that there are greater powers
That the greater part of me runs itself
That the majority the cells move my life around
As if I were not around
As if my body followed my shadow
While my shadow vanished from sight
Then I know it watches me cynically
Then I cannot comprehend it all

5

I see that I have trained my words
To move my body
To guide it safely
Through the world
While my body stays awake
And knows exactly where it is
Lost
In me

6

I see that I am here by choice
See that I do not vanish
Though I may want to
See that there is no connection
Between what I want
And what I would choose
See that I must start over
On good and evil

7

I see that there is nothing to see
See that I love you blindly
See that I walk into a fog
To find my way
Because I can see that in the fog
I cannot find my way
I see that these movements within me
Are faithful to me

8

I see the weightless clouds
I see the weightless sun
I see how easily they trace
An endless course
As if they trust in me
Here on the earth
As if they know that I
Am their words

EPILOGOS

It
That's it
It's the whole thing
It's the whole thing in a mass
It's the whole thing in a mass of difference
It's the whole thing in a mass of different people
In fear
But it's not a whole
It's nowhere near finished
It's not over
And it hasn't started
It starts
In fear
In fear like a pause
Fear of being alone
Fear of being with others
Fear of completion
Fear of incompletion
Fear of sex
Fear of death
starts everywhere
everywhere in a human being
a human being whose face
becomes a much smaller face
vanishing point
for its own vanishing
in a human being
whose inward-turned visions
return from space
as realities
   And the result
   the smashed face
   a whole of blood and pulverized bone
   of fluid from the eyes
   mixed with mucus

from various cavities
mixed with tissues and membranes
shreds of matter enamel chunks of tongue
in a sated pause devoid of images
for the mind
fear incarnate
And the process
the face destroyed
a vision like all others
a vision sent into space
a vision from the edge of visibility
rivets our gaze
so fear becomes visible
so fear can be seen in our eyes
and what is seen returns at last
to the eyes that see
to the face that smiles
to the smile that lets fear pass
and vanish into the face
and the face stays intact
the face slick as a coffin
fear incarnate animated
And the intention, meaning
to keep up to date on fear
to give yourself up to fear
like giving yourself up to a shower
to go out for fear
like going out for food
because you're hungry
to step into a coffin
like stepping into a house
fear incarnate animated activated
And the meaninglessness
that fear is there anyway
fear of being alone
fear of being with others

   fear of completion
   fear of incompletion
   fear of sex
   fear of death
The only consolation
The only coherence
that all this occurs
in one human being
that one human being
is therefore the only
each time the only
possibility
he she
must learn not
to subdue the fear
   Eccentric attempts
   to move your core
   out of yourself
   into something else
   into others
   and there
   in horror
   cruelty
   murder
   orgy
   offering
   need
   sorrow
   fury
   poverty
   blindness
   stupidity
   make conscious the leap from fear to ecstasy
   Or magical attempts
   to trust in language
   as part of biology

to trust that on its own language will
produce the necessary
feelings thoughts
if necessary new
feelings
thoughts
so we can survive fear
with our fear
intact
as we trust that our kidneys
trust in us
formulate the necessary
substances movements
if necessary new
substances
movements
so we can experience fear
with ourselves
intact
Or erotic attempts
all that unifies us
is what
divides us
in the first place death
is our only continuity
division
forever unified
in the second place life
is our particular discontinuity
unity
temporarily divided
in the third place psychic striving
total eroticism is
independent of sex
inconceivable without it
independent of death

inconceivable without it
concentrated on uniting
what is divided
forever
forced to divide
what is unified
temporarily
to be temporarily alone
to be temporarily with others
temporarily in completion
temporarily in incompletion
temporarily in sex
temporarily
not in death
to say it again
I'm afraid
The important thing is not
what we are
but what we could
well be
can be
cannot yet be
but can and will be some day
be some day
be afraid
but not afraid
of being afraid
Fear of being alone
alone with the past
alone with the great pressure of your imagination
distraction emptiness
alone with your joy your courage
your inadequate effort
alone with your song
your facts
and your freedom

alone with it all
in its discontinuous
condition
unique
incomparable
the sun
of an unobserved solar system
Fear of being with others
with others
who suddenly know
what they must not know
all that the self
does not want to know
about itself
with others
who suddenly say
that what you have said
must not be said
and if you say it again
they will leave
a threat
a shock
or with others
who just don't feel like it
and with others
who feel like too much
or with
accusation
gossip
anger
with
hope
jealousy
despair
with
demons

reasonable people
and ascetics
with everyone and everything
in its discontinuous
condition
specific
comparable to
a worn meteor
in a totally illusory solar system
Fear of completion
of habit inertia
monotonous dialogues
of recognition
repetition
conclusion
of the synthesis that is never right
of the rightness that is never honest
of the honesty that is never right
of the practical
ordered
well-organized
civilized
pattern
and of the system
of your own system
to which you cling
of the others' systems
in which you are caught up
of the system as such
magnetic
set
and all-inclusive
Fear of incompletion
of movement
space
conflict

of uncertainty
chaos
and being carefree
of superfluity
confusion
and longing
of a world that will never exist
of a world that will never be finished
of a world a mind a consciousness
that will never be caught up to
never be finished
and never exist
of what is yielding
loose
and all-exclusive
Fear of sex
of losing yourself
of losing
your dignity
prestige
your hope
of failing
losing faith
your beliefs
of being scorned and loved
needed and used
used up vanishing
of losing composure
losing your strength
your mind
your dreams
and of ecstasy
tremors
and emptiness
of vestiges
dissolution

death
and transformation
Fear of death
Fear of death
It's too much
It's impossible
It's the whole thing
That's it
It
The only thing we have
The only thing we have to do
The only thing we have to do for each other
is to say it as it is
I'm afraid
to be it as it is
to be afraid
to conquer fear with fear
and later
to conquer the fear
of informing others of
your conquered fear
it's theirs

Eccentric attempts
when a man
steps out of himself
steps out of
his daily life
his function
his situation
steps out of
his habits
his peaceful
condition
we call the process
ecstasy
when he claims

that the clouds
shoot by like pain
that the clouds
originate
in electrical charges
water vapor
flight
inside his weighted head
when he says
that he is dancing
with the Earth
hanging limp
between his legs
and when he summons
the sea
to rise up
and spurt from his organ
like a deluge
we can clearly see
that he is gripped
by love
gripped
by hatred
of fear
but how shall we invent
new feelings
how shall we invent
thoughts for the feelings
how shall we find
a technique
for understanding
a technique
for shared consciousness
a knowledge at least
of all that we don't even see
in ourselves

in the others
each other
it could be me
that stepped out of myself
Magical attempts
it could be words
that stepped out of themselves
as realities
it could be words
that swept wordlessness along
on their way through the body
it could be words
that like a fever transformed
fear to joy
it could be words
that got to the bottom
of seduction
placed their genes
in the individual
cell
grew
forced themselves through
cancer and virus
and mortalities
to the glorious stature
of antibodies
medication
salvation
it could be words
that brought grace
into the world
formulated fear
so every single fearful
person
knew that he was probably
alone in the world

was probably alone
with his fear
but never alone
with his own consciousness
of fear
of the world
it could be words
the matter we still share
with each other
the matter that can expand
the mind
and the senses
could be words
you have said
to say
the whole thing
as it is
I'm afraid
Erotic attempts
when the body
in its blind
sexual
activity
strives to be invisible
the cells are words
when the body
is lost
in it all
and lost
as it is
persists
survives
surpasses
itself
and its limits
the cells are words

when the body
is a thing
the cells are words
when the body
is convulsion
the cells are words
when the body
is muteness
action
and a stage
the cells are words
when the body
is outside
itself
and inside
another
illuminated
freed
at peace
the cells are words
a language
that tells
that the body
can waken
the dead
how
a language
that tells
that caresses
can waken
the dead
how
a language
that tells
that the abyss
between us

is filled
how
how
to let this
parallel language
grow
how
to let
the cells
in it
proliferate
find their way
to the parallel brain
how
find their way
to the parallel mouth
lips that speak
as they never
have spoken
as they always
have spoken
a kiss
how
to aim
straight
into
your heart
in any
other way than
this parallel language
that does not
exist
and never
will
I'm afraid

It starts
It starts again
It starts in me
It starts in the world
It starts in world after world
It starts far beyond the world
It starts in fear
and beyond fear
in fear subdued by fear
and fear unsubdued by fear
continues
at random as it started
in fear
and there is nothing to do but say it as it is
we're afraid
It's not random
It's not the world
It is random
It is the world
It's the whole thing in a mass of different people
It's the whole thing in a mass of difference
It's the whole thing in a mass
It's the whole thing
That's it
It